Preaching in Jamaican Seasons

Preaching in Jamaican Seasons

Devon Dick

WIPF & STOCK · Eugene, Oregon

Arawak publications
Kingston • Jamaica • The Caribbean

© 2022 by Devon Dick
All rights reserved. Published 2022

25 24 23 22
d c b a

NATIONAL LIBRARY OF JAMAICA CATALOGUING-IN-PUBLICATION DATA
Name: Dick, Devon, author.
Title: Preaching in Jamaican seasons / Devon Dick.
Description: Kingston, Jamaica : Arawak publications, 2022.
  | Includes bibliographical references.
Identifier: ISBN 9789768282477 (pbk).
Subjects: LCSH: Preaching. | Expository preaching. | Topical preaching.
Classification: DDC 251 – dc23.

Credits
Back cover image: Congregation in a song of praise, at the National Church Service to mark the start of Civil Service Week, held at the Tarrant Baptist Church in Kingston, 17 November 2013.

This edition licensed by special permission from Arawak publications

Wipf & Stock
An Imprint of Wipf and Stock Publishers
199 W. 8th Ave., Suite 3
Eugene, OR 97401

www.wipfandstock.com

PAPERBACK ISBN: 978-1-6667-6322-5
HARDCOVER ISBN: 978-1-6667-6323-2
EBOOK ISBN: 978-1-6667-6324-9

Book design by Annika Lewinson-Morgan
Set in Optima 11/13.25pt with Cinzel and Cinzel Decorative

Contents

List of Figures / *iv*
Foreword – *Revd Merlyn Hyde Riley* / *v*
Preface / *vii*
Acknowledgments / *x*
Introduction / *xiii*

Chapter One: Preaching During a Pandemic / *1*
    "Take Loving to Another Level" (9 August 2020) / *1*
    "I Am a Jamaican Christian" (2 August 2020) / *4*
    "Listen for the Voice of God" (26 July 2020) / *10*
    "Use the Opportunities of Youthfulness" (19 July 2020) / *16*
    "Start a Moral Revolution" (12 July 2020) / *22*
    "Pray to the Lord" (5 July 2020) / *29*

Chapter Two: Presidential Proclamations / *37*
    "Living in Partnership" (2018 JBU Assembly) / *37*
    "Witnessing Fervently" (2018 JBU Assembly) / *47*
    "Giving Freely" (2017 JBU Assembly) / *57*

Chapter Three: Special Occasion Sermons / *69*
    "Neutral on Nothing" – Ordination of Revd Derrick Saddler
    (5 September 2019) / *69*
    "Do the Right Thing" – 55th Anniversary of the JTA
    (18 August 2019) / *77*
    "Eat with Sinners" – 60th Anniversary of JTA Co-op Credit Union
    (20 January 2019) / *84*
    "A Little Wine" – 100th Anniversary of Red Stripe Beer
    (8 July 2018) / *89*
    "Celebration" (1989 JBU Assembly) / *93*

Chapter Four: Home-Going Homilies / **97**

    Funeral for Maud Daley, Deacon (31 July 2020): *"The Lord's My Shepherd"* / **97**

    Funeral for Deryck Brown, Deacon (28 February 2020): *"I Am Brown and Comely"* / **102**

    Funeral for Luther Gibbs, Founding Pastor (6 July 2019): *"The Victorious Will Inherit This"* / **106**

    Funeral for Violet Mosse-Brown, Oldest Woman in the World (7 October 2017): *"Praise Be to the God of All Comfort"* / **112**

    Funeral for Aaron Jordan Miller, A Teenager (10 September 2016): *"The Lord Is Close to the Brokenhearted"* / **115**

    Funeral for Kayla Richardson, A Child (11 August 2008): *"His Wisdom Is Profound, His Power Is Vast"* / **120**

Epilogue – Evangelistic Exhortation: "Repent and Be Baptized" (3 May 2015) / **128**

Afterword – *Revd Judith Johnson-Grant* / **132**

Bibliography / **135**

LIST OF FIGURES

Figure 1: Devon Dick, Pastor, with shield over face to help prevent the spread of the COVID-19 virus / xxviii

Figure 2: "No Mask, No Service" sign at the entrance of the Church of the Transfiguration, Kingston / 35

Figure 3: Devon Dick preaching at 2018 JBU Assembly / 36

Figure 4: Derrick Saddler, Ordinand, and Devon Dick, Preacher, at Ordination Service, Moses Baker Baptist Church, St Thomas / 74

Figure 5: Congregation at Boulevard Baptist Church for 60th Anniversary of the JTA Co-operative Credit Union / 81

Figure 6: Luther Gibbs, CD, MA, Founding Pastor, Boulevard Baptist Church / 107

Foreword

I am pleased to have been asked by the Revd Dr Devon Dick to write the Foreword to this book of sermons. He must be commended for undertaking this publication as there is a dearth of published sermons within the Caribbean, and therefore a veritable treasure of sermon resources would have been lost over time. This book will undoubtedly help to fill a long existing gap, and generations to come will be able to benefit from the liberating and transformative impact of the word of God proclaimed through these pages.

This work reaffirms the view that preaching is a unique ministry grounded in the will and purpose of God, in Christ Jesus, through the witness of the Spirit. In God's wisdom, it is the primary way in which the Good News is to be shared in the world. There is simply no authentic equivalent to the fundamental practice of proclamation in human civilization. Indeed, there can be no real and viable substitute for it.

Detectable in the sermons in this work are a strong social consciousness, a prophetic mandate, and a commitment to speaking truth to power whilst challenging the institutional and structural ills of society. At the same time, it is instructive that this book of sermons begins with the theme of love and ends with the call to repent and be baptized, for at the heart of the proclamation of the Gospel is sharing the love of God and embracing the Good News of the Gospel of Jesus Christ.

Readers will be struck by the Revd Dr Dick's relatable and conversational tone, and the honesty and humanity coming through the pages. His commitment to activism, and his embracing of human dignity, justice and human flourishing give his book of sermons authenticity and credibility.

Revd Dr Dick, quite generously, takes the time in this relatively brief publication to identify and celebrate the work of other distinguished Caribbean preachers. By referencing these works, he demonstrates an appreciation for the relevance of a historical and Caribbean frame in the shaping of preachers and preaching in the Caribbean, where the social, political, economic, moral and spiritual milieu provides a rich context within which to interpret and proclaim the word of God. The consistent threads in the themes he highlights in these works, and which run throughout this publication of sermons, certainly underscore the continuing relevance and enduring nature of the word of God proclaimed across time and space.

The publication is relevant, pragmatic and theologically sound, which will make it appealing to the average person who needs to hear a word from the Lord in simple understandable language, to the preacher searching for sermon ideas, and to the student of theology studying hermeneutics.

— **Revd Merlyn Hyde Riley**
Immediate Past President of the Jamaica Council of Churches
Acting General Secretary, Jamaica Baptist Union

Preface

On Monday, 20 April 2020, I started this compilation of sermons, the day which marked the end of my tenure writing a weekly column for *The Gleaner*. This is a collection of twenty-one sermons, which were delivered between 1989 and 2020.

The seed of publishing a book of sermons was planted in my subconscious in 1985 by Revd J.J. Williams, then pastor of the Richmond Vale Circuit of Baptist Churches, St Thomas, better known as a choir director, musician and singer par excellence. Williams, handed me a printed copy of the sermon he preached after a "special commissioning service" to mark my departure from the Morant Bay Circuit of Baptist Churches, St Thomas, in order to start pastoral ministry through Fletcher's Grove Baptist, Sandy Bay, Hanover. He remains the only preacher to have ever given me a printed copy of a sermon directly related to me. There is a place for sharing written sermons.

Lately, I have started to follow that example, and I give printed copies of sermons I have preached to persons directly related to those sermons. The first recipient was Deacon Hyacinth Brown. I gave her a copy of the sermon I preached on 28 February 2020 at the funeral service for Deryck Brown, her husband; it is included in this compilation.

Furthermore, when I was chairman of the media commission of the Jamaica Baptist Union (JBU), I conceptualized compiling sermons to mark 50 years of *Christ for Today*, a JBU-produced religious radio programme aired on Radio Jamaica. In writing the Foreword to that work, "Baptist Preaching in Jamaica: Celebrating Christ for Today (1964-2014)", I had expressed the hope "that more Baptist preachers will publish their sermons" (2015, p. vii). This collection is an expression of my effort to practise what I preach.

Most of my sermons in this publication were delivered subsequent to my appointment as pastor of Boulevard Baptist Church, St Andrew, on 1 October 1990. One sermon in this collection was written while I was pastor of Fletcher's Grove Baptist Church, Sandy Bay, Hanover, but coincidentally was preached at Boulevard Baptist during the

1989 JBU Assembly. Therefore, so much of what has evolved into these sermons was learned, refined, confirmed and verified mainly among the saints at Boulevard Baptist Church.

For me, preaching a sermon is the most difficult aspect of pastoral ministry. It is harder than praying to God; harder than counselling someone; harder than administering the church's affairs; harder than visitation ministry; harder than giving a lecture; harder than conducting a Sunday School class or teaching a Bible study session. Preaching is challenging, complex and demanding, because preaching is really saying, "Thus saith the Lord." It is being a spokesperson for God, discerning the mind of God and then declaring the counsel of God with passion, boldness and conviction. Preaching is not easy because the preacher must hear from God in order to explain the holy scriptures for faith and practice to the congregation. It is not easy to get it right all the time on behalf of God. That makes preaching so difficult, because it is hard to attain anything near perfection. Only Jesus was a perfect preacher. So, I am acutely aware of my limitations as a preacher.

Additionally, the expectations of the congregants of the preacher are very high; the people are filled with a desire for the gospel truth, expecting that their genuine needs will be met, wanting answers for their problems, and needing guidance for decisions to be made. There is also the need for comfort in times of crisis, illness, sickness, accident, tragedy and death. Besides, some come to be motivated to higher heights and deeper depths in their walk with God. Some come to celebrate their faithfulness to God and their success in life. Therefore, like Paul, a preacher has to take the stance that "tu di piipl dem we wiik mi ton wiik tu, so dat mi kuda elp dem fi biliiv iina Jizas Krais. So bies pan ou piipl liv, mi chienj ou mi liv so dat mi wuda du aal we mi kuda du fi elp siev som a dem" (1 Kor 9:22 Di Jamiekan Nyuu Testament). A preacher has to be all things to all congregants, meeting various and competing needs in one sermon.

Moreover, taste in sermons is like appreciation for beauty; it is always in the eye of the beholder. Many individuals have asked me for a copy of a sermon, or enquired whether I would be publishing a book of sermons at any point. Some members of the clergy have expressed appreciation for my preaching, such as Roman Catholic priest Revd Fr Donald Chambers who in autographing a copy of his book of sermons *Transformed by the Deep* (2017) wrote, "Thanks for your inspirational preaching...". Additionally, almost every time I told

Preface

someone I was going on sabbatical leave (1 March to 30 June, 2020), the usual question was whether I was going to publish a book. These and other events have given me the impetus to publish a book of sermons.

So, what am I hoping to accomplish with this publication? This compilation of sermons is offered so that they can be read, and hopefully be a source of comfort to persons who are afflicted, confront those who need to change, and challenge all to a commitment to God as revealed in Jesus, the Christ, and empowered by the Spirit. It is my desire that in reading these sermons each person will hear a clear message from God that can be applied to the lived experience.

It is further hoped that these sermons, when read, will come to life again, aided by the working of the Holy Spirit, and teach and guide us into righteousness. It is planting a seed in a person's life, knowing that it will accomplish that which God wills, as He gives it the increase beyond anything I could dream of or envision.

Finally, a written sermon has a voice of its own. Hopefully, readers will hear the prophetic voice, the therapeutic voice and the teaching voice in these homiletical formulations and, more importantly, I hope they will hear the voice of our Saviour Jesus, the Christ, speaking to our hearts and minds.

Acknowledgments

It is impossible to publish a book unaided. One has to rely on so many people for assistance in producing any publication. This work is no exception.

Moreover, no matter how comprehensive a list of acknowledgements is, there will always be some people who are not mentioned because they are not known by the writer, such as the reviewers of the manuscript and the workers at the printer whom this author did not meet. I would like to thank these invisible people whose handiwork has made this publication visible. Furthermore, in a compilation such as this which covers a journey of thirty plus years, some persons who encouraged and facilitated this work have been forgotten. I say thank you to these people also.

I would like to say thank you to all who read this manuscript meticulously, or parts of it, and made it a better product, such as Revd Dr Burchel Taylor, retired JBU pastor; Althea Meade Hadjuk and Karen Robertson Henry, my dear friends from our university days (1982-85). Their task was made even more difficult by having to wade through thoughts and sermons which were not properly connected.

My heartfelt thanks to the Revd Merlyn Hyde Riley, first female president of the Jamaica Council of Churches and acting general secretary of the Jamaica Baptist Union, who graciously wrote the Foreword, and to the Revd Judith Johnson-Grant, pastor of the St Margaret's Bay Circuit of Baptist Churches, Portland, and my former aide when I was president of the JBU. She kindly wrote the Afterword, even while doing her postgraduate studies. Their benevolent expressions were only surpassed by their compassionate hearts.

I would like to express my gratitude to those who loaned or gave me books of sermons, such as Revd Dr Garnett Roper, president of the Jamaica Theological Seminary (*Preach It, Journey to the Promised Land,* and *Thus Says the Lord: Responding to the Resurgence of Empire*); Revd Dr Paul Gardner, past president of the Moravian Church in Jamaica and former president of the Unity Board of the worldwide Moravian Church (*Seedtime and Harvest*); Dr Ishmael Robertson, founding member of Hope United Church (*Transformed by the Deep*); and Revd Dr Glenroy

Acknowledgments

Lalor, pastor of the Bethel Baptist Church (*Caribbean Pulpit*). Without their generosity, the Introduction to this book would be poorer.

My sincere thanks to the late Revd Clement Gayle, my homiletics tutor and Baptist warden at the United Theological College of the West Indies (UTCWI), who took me under his wing for special treatment, and who had a great impact on my preaching through his insightful and piercing comments. Thank you also to the president of the UTCWI, Revd Dr Oral Thomas, for his support of this project.

I am deeply grateful to the Boulevard Baptist Church, in association with the JBU, which facilitated my first sabbatical leave, which lasted for four months. This time off allowed for the reflection and renewal I needed in order to undertake this task. In addition, our beloved JBU gave a monetary contribution toward this leave. A special thank you also to Minerva Powell, Boulevard Baptist Church's administrative assistant who willingly re-typed the oldest sermon in this collection.

I would also like to express my thanks to many churches where I heard the Gospel preached for a significant period in my life, such as Airy Castle Methodist Church, St Thomas; Maggotty United Church, St Elizabeth; Grace Missionary Church and Grants Pen United Pentecostal Church, both in St Andrew.

I am deeply grateful to the late Deaconess Joyce Channer who was audibly supportive when I preached my first sermon at an evening service at Mamby Park Baptist Church, St Andrew, in 1978, and to the late Revd Joseph Edwards, pastor of Mamby Park Baptist Church, who opened his pulpit to me for my maiden sermon. Unfortunately, the delivery was so bad that I was not asked to preach at Mamby Park again for another two years.

My heartfelt thanks to Cardovan Jackson, my friend and colleague in the mathematics department at Morant Bay High School, St Thomas. He was very encouraging in word and deed when I preached my first sermon in a morning service at Leith Hall Baptist Church, St Thomas, in 1979. I also want to thank the pastor of the Morant Bay Circuit of Baptist Churches, Revd Stivel Crossman, who for two years (1979-81) gave me great latitude and monthly opportunities to declare the Word of God. This aided my development as a preacher.

My heartfelt appreciation goes to the many members who faithfully listened to my preaching over these many years – at Boulevard Baptist since 1990; at Fletcher's Grove Baptist Church (1985-90); when Mt Pelier class house became a church in 1987; at Buff Bay Circuit of Baptist Churches (1981-82) when I was a student pastor; at East

Queen Street Circuit, and at Denham Town Baptist, Kingston (1980-81) where I was assigned by Revd Dr Horace Russell, then pastor at the East Queen Street Circuit. These saints of Christ listened attentively as I presented God as revealed in Jesus the Christ and empowered by the Holy Spirit, and encouraged a commitment to the triune God. There are many persons indeed who have helped to mould me as a preacher since I started preaching in 1979. Many have offered critical comments which have encouraged me over the years. Thank you.

I would like to thank my publisher Arawak publications and her team. Arawak published *Enduring Advocacy for a Better Jamaica: A Collection of Conversations* (2019). And as the saying goes "every good turn deserves another".

My sincere thanks to my sponsors: TIP Friendly Society, through its president Ray Howell, was the first to respond to a request for financial help. My heartfelt thanks also to my son Duvaughn Dick, who through his company Advantage Physical Therapy & Rehabilitation, provided sponsorship. In addition, thanks for sponsorship from the Jamaica Teachers' Association through its secretary general, Byron Farquharson; Jamaica Broilers through its chairman Robert Levy; Victoria Mutual through its CEO Courtney Campbell; and Jamaica Money Market Brokers through chairman of the Foundation Patricia Sutherland.

I must express my deepest gratitude to Mary Elizabeth, my wife since 1985, the person who has listened to more of my sermons in person than anyone else, and the one who has been my sounding board and chief advisor on giving more "oomph" to the sermons. My son Duvaughn would be next in line in hearing more of my preaching than others. My eldest child Deon escaped many of my sermons for twelve years while she studied at Florida International University, then at Duke University and finally at the University of Miami. Dana, my younger daughter, missed four years of my sermons while studying at Cass Business School, London, and working in the United Kingdom. Nevertheless, they would offer critical support and appreciation as they continued to watch the sermons streamed live from a great distance in the last few years.

Above all, thanks be to God who in His uncanny wisdom called, selected and equipped me to be a preacher, in spite of being the son of a mother who was a dressmaker and a father who was a shoemaker. Thanks be to Almighty God who entrusted me to proclaim the person of Jesus, the Lord and Saviour of the world, as the central subject, object and foundation of preaching (1 Cor 3:11).

Introduction

The aim of this book is to offer sermons preached by a Jamaican in a Jamaican context at different seasons for the edification of saints and to the glory of God. It is hoped that it will be a small contribution to biblical expository preaching for the Jamaican situation. Consistent with the sermons being preached by a Jamaican in a Jamaican setting, all quotations from the Scriptures in the Preface and Introduction will be in the Jamaican language, taken from *Di Jamiekan Nyuu Testament* (JNT).

Delineate This Work

The title of this book, *Preaching in Jamaican Seasons*, is informed by the Pauline injunction to "priich Gad wod an mek shuor se yu aalwiez redi fi priich. Ef di taim rait ar it no rait, priich it siem wie. Yu afi shuo di piipl dem di rang we dem a du an put dem iina dem plies kaaz dem a sin. Yu mos tek taim wid dem wen yu a tiich dem an push dem fi du wa rait" (2 Tim 4:2). Paul desired that Timothy, his young ministry partner, proclaim the divine truth. This was an urgent undertaking to be done earnestly and passionately and Timothy was to seek every opportunity whether it was convenient or inopportune, and whether people were receptive to the message or not. This was a full-time calling and commitment. Accordingly, there was intentionality in titling this book by grounding it in a biblical text (2 Tim 4:2).

This collection of sermons consists of the first six sermons preached on a Sunday morning during the coronavirus disease 2019 (COVID-19) pandemic, just after I completed my sabbatical on 30 June 2020. The COVID-19 pandemic, with the attendant lockdown of economy and country, ushered in a new normal. The pandemic also exposed the existing inadequate living conditions of many and the excessive privileges of the few. Therefore, God's mouthpiece had to address the existential conditions. The prevailing issue in Jamaica at the time of compiling this book is the pandemic. Then, there are three sermons preached while I was president of the Jamaica Baptist Union (2016-18) addressing denominational, national and international issues. In addition, there are "special occasion sermons", such as those delivered when special groups celebrated significant events at a Sunday morning worship service at Boulevard Baptist. In addition, there are six funeral sermons which located eulogies of the deceased in the Bible. Finally, there is an evangelistic sermon, a call to salvation in order to live a life with advantage, meaning and purpose. These sermons were preached at different seasons – some celebratory and some sorrowful, but all challenging us to have a right relationship with God and our fellow human beings.

Sermon Anthologies in Jamaica

There is a dearth of published sermons preached by our local ministers, and there are many reasons for this, including a lack of confidence in their preaching and writing skills, too little popular demand for such publications, a lack of funding to cover the cost of publishing, the absence of the critical mass needed to make such a venture profitable, not enough appreciation of Jamaican sermons in seminaries, a lack of time and perhaps even a lack of discipline needed for such an undertaking. Furthermore, some preachers are perfectionists and are waiting on the perfect sermon or perfect time to publish. Some are afraid of criticism, whether fair or unfair, and published sermons are easier to scrutinize than those listened to from the pews. It could also be that preachers think that others who are "better preachers" should do it. Whatever the reasons, there is a paucity of published sermons by Jamaicans within the Jamaican context.

There are, however, some notable exceptions. *Journey to the Promised Land* (2019) is a collection of synod sermons delivered from 1979 to 2000 by the outspoken 12th Bishop of the Anglican Diocese of Jamaica and the Cayman Islands, Neville W. deSouza. During Jamaica's turbulent socioeconomic and political time, he advocated for the church to be aligned with the class of people who were exploited rather than the class that comprised the elites who acquired more than they needed.

Also in 2019, Burchell Taylor, former president of the Jamaica Baptist Union and Caribbean Baptist Fellowship, produced *The Best of the Attitudes: The Jesus Way*, which is a meditation on the Beatitudes in the Gospel according to Matthew. He reinforced some truths and insights about the Beatitudes. He offered the Beatitudes as a model to help in character formation.

The year before, in 2018, God spoke through the president of the

Introduction

Jamaica Theological Seminary, Garnett Roper, who announced the publication of his book *Thus Says the Lord*. It was an assemblage of 35 sermons commemorating 40 years of Sunday morning radio sermons on the "Grace Hour Broadcast". Roper explored the minor prophets and Daniel, and showed that their voices were not obsolete or immaterial. Furthermore, he demonstrated that their message, in the various contexts, had as much relevance then as it does now, as there was the continued need for social justice in our time as well. These prophets challenged people to faithfulness in the pursuit of the divine purpose in the face of the exploitative and encompassing kingdoms and empires in which they lived.

There were also his monographs, "Who God Bless, No Man Curse" (2016) and "This Is the Year of Jubilee" (2012). In the former, he explored blessedness not as material prosperity only, or mainly, but more as human flourishing based on God's goodness, generosity and greatness. In the latter, Roper celebrated Jamaica's 50 years of independence from British colonial imperialism. In that publication, the biblical concept of Jubilee was explored for its relevance and implications for Jamaica.

Then there was Donald Chambers' *Transformed by the Deep* (2017), a compilation of 90 sermons, speeches and presentations delivered by Chambers, former priest of the influential Sts Peter and Paul Catholic Church, Kingston, during his 25 years as a priest. He proclaimed that every person can be transformed by the love of God.

In 2015, there was *Baptist Preaching in Jamaica: Celebrating Christ for Today (1964-2014)*, which showcased the state of preaching in the JBU. The varied sermons reflected issues which both nation and church were facing.

S.U. Hastings, the first Jamaican appointed as a bishop of the Moravian Church (1961) produced *These Fifty Years* (1991), a book of 50 sermons to mark 50 years of ordained ministry. They were a potpourri of sermons which gave an indication of national and international events and the depth of his concerns.

Horace Russell, first Caribbean president of UTCWI, produced *Five Words of Love* which is an exposition of Jan 3:16: "Kaa, you si, Gad lov di worl so moch dat im gi op im wan dege-dege Bwai Pikni, so enibadi we chos iina im naa go ded bot a-go liv fi eva". These five sermons were delivered while Russell was pastor of East Queen Street Baptist Church (1983).

There were other publications that were not produced exclusively for the Jamaican context, but were Caribbean or for the diaspora. Clement Gayle, Jamaican-born homiletics lecturer, and William Watty, Dominican-born Methodist minister and then President of UTCWI, edited a book of sermons entitled *A Caribbean Pulpit* (1983). This anthology contained a cross section of Caribbean preaching addressing various social, political and spiritual issues such as "The Place of Women in Christ's Church" (pp. 12-19); "The Revolution in Grenada" (pp. 23-28); and "What is the Mission of the Church?" (pp. 29-33). Also, in 1981, in *From Shore to Shore: Soundings in Caribbean Theology*, Watty published several speeches and one sermon, "The Creator of the Young Culture" (pp. 62-68). This sermon was delivered at a service of thanksgiving concluding Culturama celebrations at UTCWI.

For the diaspora, Russell published *8 Eight Pathways to Happiness: Living the Be-Attitudes* (2012), a devotional book for Lent based on the Beatitudes and preached at First Baptist Church of Philadelphia, USA. Russell also published *Ten Reasons for Living: Studies in the Lord's Prayer* (2011), a collection of ten sermons on the Lord's Prayer preached in the aftermath of the September 11 attacks in New York and Washington, DC, and which offered Jesus as the only hope.

All these publications demonstrate vividly the importance of preaching in a worship service.

CENTRALITY OF PREACHING IN WORSHIP SERVICES

Preaching is central to Baptist worship, witness and work; hence most Baptist churches have the pulpit in the centre of the altar to symbolize the centrality of the preached word of God. The sermon or "message" or "Word", for many, is the climax of the congregational worship experience of prayer, praise, petition, reading of scriptures, and announcements of opportunities to worship God and engage in His service. It is the chief event. Preaching has a rightful preeminent place because God created the world by speaking, which shows the importance and power of the spoken word. Jesus' most well-known sermon was declared on a mountain (Matt. 5-7); Jonah was commissioned to be a preacher to the people of Nineveh who needed to repent (1:1-2; 3:1); the Prophets declared "thus saith the Lord", making known the will of God to the children of Israel (Exod. 4:21-23; Isa. 48:16-17; Jer. 33:1-4); and after Pentecost, Peter preached the salvation history of God to thousands with great effect (Acts 2:14-41).

Introduction

Given the essence of the word there is no adequate substitute for preaching as described in the scriptures. Due to the very nature of their material and content, the best way to communicate these doctrines is through preaching. The nature of biblical truth and biblical theology requires preaching to best communicate those truths and theology. Dance, song and drama are not adequate substitutes to preaching; although these expressions of worship can enhance preaching, preaching ought to be the primary communication tool.

The centrality of preaching the Bible ought to be the major source with no equal, not tradition, not the testimony of the saints, nor science, not supernatural or experiential spirituality, singspiration or season of prayers. However, not everyone within and without share the view that preaching ought to be the mainstay of Christian worship, and more voices are claiming that preaching is vastly overrated.

Preaching Challenged

Pride of place for preaching is challenged with some congregants demanding more time for praise and worship, choruses and less time for preaching. Furthermore, there is impatience with so-called "long sermons" that delve into scriptures, examine the demands of God and call for sacrificial living and simple lifestyle. Many want short sermons with comedy, and prosperity pep rallies. So, soundbites and sloganeering are in vogue and preaching is a victim of the new technology-driven communication culture.

Some hearers want a type of preaching which offers signs; they at times demand a sign like a wicked generation (Matt. 16:4) or want more opportunity to shout loudly, like the worshippers of Baal (1 Kings 18:26). Some are attracted to preachers who proffer vain repetitions and many words, like heathens (Matt. 6:8), and then there are those who desire sermons that are topical without being scriptural, which takes preaching into the realm of social commentary. Some love sermons that are superficial, wherein Jesus is neglected and the Scriptures ignored, and the preacher is no more than a motivational speaker uttering wishful thinking. These congregants succeed by their own strength and determination only.

There is also a following for preachers who will "declare and decree", who will encourage people to "name it and claim it" and "speak over one's own life", and who will promote "sowing a seed" to spur God to provide health and wealth for worshippers. This type of preaching is hardly ever about church unity, strength in the face of persecution, or courage to embrace sacrificial service. It is self-centred worship, and they are making God in their image to do their bidding or pretending and proclaiming that they are "god".

There is also pushback against preaching perceived as finger pointing, and against being "preached at". People prefer instructional sermons that are not judgmental. They want the dialogue and not the monologue of preaching. American pop singer Madonna with her Roman Catholic upbringing reflects the mood of many with an aversion to being preached at in her song "Papa Don't Preach" (1986), which deals with the issue of teenage pregnancy. In the song, Madonna assumes the role of a daughter who has messed up her life after ignoring her father's counsel and now needs good advice, but she states emphatically, "Papa don't preach, I'm in trouble deep / Papa don't preach, I've been losing sleep…." She wanted comfort without challenge; she wanted a priest for absolution and not a prophet to condemn her. She does not want to hear from a preacher. She wants only understanding and support for her intentions going forward, and not a sermon to analyse her behaviour, prescribe certain correct actions, and to tell of the consequences of the choices available based on Christian principles.

Some even dare to want God to help them cover their tracks as exemplified by Christopher Martin's song "Cheaters Prayer" (2017). This Jamaican crooner in a dancehall style states: "Oh Lord, don't let me cheat on my girlfriend / But Lord if you can't stop me from cheating / Just don't let me get caught / No, no, no…" God is expected to be a conspirator in a cheating affair. God is to do Martin's will, while Martin does not have to do what is right in the sight of God.

Furthermore, there is frustration and impatience with traditional preaching with its typical structure of a main point and three supporting points. Dr Carol Tomlin, cofounder of an independent non-denominational group of churches, Restoration Fellowship Ministries, states that deductive preaching is "based on the Enlightenment rationalistic hermeneutical paradigm…. Meaning of texts are conveyed to listeners in a linear fashion and sermons progress sequentially with clear argumentation concluding with specific applications for the listening audience, a seemingly monologic sermon style, which affirms the authoritarian role of the preacher, disconnected from the audience" (Tomlin 2018: 59). Her preference is for an inductive style which transforms listeners from passive recipients to active participants.

Introduction

The departure from traditional preaching was graphically displayed by the flamboyant, well-known Jamaican televangelist Andrew Scott who used sound and visual effects, and other special effects on the local cable channel, Mercy and Truth Ministries (MTM). It was not unusual to witness him healing someone with special effects representing the healing travelling through the congregant's body. In addition, when he is praying for the person and before he pushes that person backwards to the ground, there are powerful sounds akin to lightning and thunder. Furthermore, if he were praying for a heart problem, then a pulsating heart was displayed, or if the prayer were for back pain, then the x-ray image of a spine separated from a human body would appear (viewed 22 April 2020). These preaching aids could be indicative of a waning interest in the power of traditional preaching. The question is whether a preacher can shun these manmade aids and marketing techniques and still find preaching fulfilling and effective by relying solely on God for the results. Another issue for preachers to work through is whether preaching for them is a matter of performance, rather than proclamation that is Christocentric that also embraces the triune nature of the revealed Word.

Then there are the cynics, sceptics and agnostics who point fingers at the waning credibility of preachers, but even if the lifestyle of the preacher is not perfect, this does not mean the preacher should abandon the calling, because the preacher is also preaching to himself or herself toward maturing in the Christian faith. The preachers' effectiveness is not entirely dependent on the general public's trust in them. Additionally, some people are unfairly critical of and openly abusive to many preachers. They define the relevance of preaching based on how it fits into their partisan political and ideological agendas.

Some try to demoralize preachers by highlighting the lower numbers of Jamaicans identifying with the Church in Jamaica when compared to the immediate post-emancipation era. In 1943 approximately 90 per cent of Jamaicans stated that they were affiliated with a church, but succeeding decades until the 1990s saw a significant fall with 800,000 Jamaicans out of 2.5 million no longer being affiliated with a church (Dick 2002: 6). Generally, preachers are not witnessing a bumper harvest of souls.

Preaching in Jamaican Seasons

A Comeback through the Art of Preaching

Preaching can make a comeback aided and abetted by a recommitment to the art of preaching. David Kuck, minister in the Evangelical Lutheran Church in the USA, and the then lecturer in homiletics at UTCWI, filled a gap in 2007 with the pioneering work *Preaching in the Caribbean: Building Up a People for Mission*, which concerned the art of preaching in the Caribbean context. Kuck posited that the preacher must be relevant to the context of the congregation in order to be effective in mission. He perceived the preacher as a facilitator of the transforming conversation between scripture and the saints. He outlined the principles of preaching, the role of the preacher, and how to prepare and deliver a sermon. He also outlined how to preach in the different seasons of life, such as at funerals, weddings and other special occasions, and to children and youth.

Kuck (2007) offers six basic convictions about preaching, which are all worthy of emulation:

1. Preaching should be an exposition of a biblical text. There is a place for topical preaching, but the "people of God generally need to hear, week by week, the actual biblical content" (2007: xiii).

2. Good preaching needs to arise from a solid theological understanding of the nature of the word of God. In this approach, law is understood not so much as a set of rules, but rather as an uncovering of the human condition in the presence of God, while the gospel is understood as God's gracious action on behalf of humanity in its plight.

3. Preaching must have a clear goal in mind. It is not to describe the human condition only, or to proclaim the grace of God only, but also to provide the hearers with a sense of what the "outcome of this message will be in their faith and life" (2007: xiii). It is to drive Christians to mission and service.

4. Good preaching must not only speak to the personal comforts of the people, but must also address church, and social and political realities with the liberating word of God.

5. Good preaching can embrace different styles and forms. This flexibility is allowed once the scriptural basis is solid, the analysis of the human condition and proclamation of the good news are clear, and the goal of the sermon is well defined.

Introduction

6. Good preaching must be pragmatic, relating to the lives of the hearers. It cannot be abstract and foreign to their experience. The hearers must feel that the preacher has addressed their context. The examples, illustrations and stories must be transferable to their hurts and hopes so that their lives can be transformed. The preacher needs an "informed imagination" and ought to use biblical and contemporary imagery to make the message real, meaningful, persuasive and impactful.

Might I add that good preaching is supposed to glorify God. The preacher must be hidden behind the Cross of Calvary and must put the focus on God.

Prerequisites for Jamaican Preachers

Furthermore, there are specific prerequisites for preachers in Jamaica, such as an understanding of the heritage of Jamaica. The preacher should be well informed about the peculiarities and heritage of the location. Good preaching should be contextual. This shows that preachers relate to their setting and their history.

In addition to the local history, a preacher must understand the history of the Church in Jamaica. The preacher should be versed in the knowledge of the role the collective Church has played in the spread of Christianity, economic empowerment, social relief, educational advancement, political peace and values formation among the people, and also the impact of Black Jamaicans in the formulation of an Afro-Jamaican identity and the Church's attendant role in emancipation and political independence.

Moreover, the preacher ought to know that Christianity arrived in Jamaica in the fifteenth century. It was a colonialism oriented church which came to be chaplain to the colonizers, and only latterly developed a mission toward persons of colour, and even then, there was a minimalist focus of saving the soul while ignoring the oppressive and dehumanizing slavery conditions of the people. Thereafter, the focus was on personal piety, so that the enslaved people would believe themselves to be honest and hardworking on the plantations, instead of the message being holistic and empowering to help the colonized confront the principalities and powers of the empire and throw off the shackles of slavery.

However, the word is liberating. The hypocrisy of employing the word as a tool of oppression was exposed, criticized and challenged by preachers of African descent, preachers such as Baptist deacon Sam Sharpe, now a national hero, who offered a different understanding of God and interpreted scripture as a means to liberate both mind and body. This tradition was continued by other pastors and preachers, such as national heroes Paul Bogle and George William Gordon who advocated equality of all and demanded justice for everyone.

Nevertheless, in the 1860s all mainline churches were on the side of Governor Edward Eyre the oppressor and anti-Bogle governor. Many mainline preachers have a history of supporting the status quo. In the 1960s, the Walter Rodney Riots occurred. Guyanese Walter Rodney, a University of the West Indies lecturer, was declared persona non grata by the Hugh Shearer JLP government. His books were also banned. After a meeting between Shearer, the then prime minister, and church leaders, mainline preachers were warned not to say anything in their sermons against the government in the interest of national security (*The Daily Gleaner*, 5 December 1968, p. 1, cited in Dick, *Rebellion to Riot*, 2002: 95). This attitude continued with the organizers of the National Prayer Breakfast being cautious not to use scripture that could be offensive to politicians (May 2020 discussion). Some preachers have been known to give unquestioned loyalty and obedience to political parties and to become parrots for governments, giving assurances of peace, prophesying declines in the numbers of murders, promising electoral success for favourite politicians, and the disappearance of COVID-19 by September 2020. Unfortunately, too many preachers have a bias toward supporting the governing authorities, being quick to justify that position by quoting Romans 13 which encouraged obedience to whichever government is in authority at a given moment, while ignoring Revelation 13 which called upon the Christians to resist the political beast represented there.

Before we are preachers, we are women and men of free will. As preachers, our personal and pastoral choices must be informed by the word we preach. We must be vigilant not to succumb to the temptation of choosing might over right, of acting in the interest of the powerful over the powerless, of the greedy over the needy. A preacher has to make the choice of whether to behave preferentially toward those people who are poor, oppressed and marginalized, or to uphold those who benefit in perpetuity from oppression. The Jamaican preacher

Introduction

cannot be a silent partner in the company trading in evil, wickedness, injustice and inequality. The Jamaican preacher cannot be just an observer of the persistent poverty, the senseless slaughter of citizens, including women and children, and the pervasive sexual slackness in society. The preacher ought to agitate for legislative changes based on equality of all and justice for all. The preacher is a mouthpiece for God who is always on the side of the righteous and the downtrodden.

The Jamaican preacher ought also to be sensitive to the effects of the legacy of slavery and indentured servitude on the psyche of many Jamaicans who feel innately inferior to foreigners, and who feel a deep-seated internalized racism toward themselves and each other resulting in high homicide rates.

After 1962, the year Jamaica gained political independence, people of colour found confidence to become religious leaders, managing city churches which were abandoned by most expatriates. Subsequently, these leaders established religious radio programmes, secondary schools, children's homes, homes for the aged, and training centres. In addition, Jamaicans themselves became missionaries, reversing the trend of Jamaica receiving missionaries. It would be useful for preachers to be conversant with this history and ethos, enabling us to preach with sensitivity toward our hearers and to interpret scripture to address pertinent and urgent issues of our situation and nation.

The Jamaican preacher needs to be gender aware since women are facing challenges of discrimination, violence and assault. Jamaica has never had a female Bank of Jamaica governor or female minister of finance, for example, and there is inequality seen in the number of appointed senators to the upper house. Baptists came to Jamaica in 1783 and the founder of the work, George Liele, had twenty-four elders with twelve being females, but the Jamaican Baptist Church itself did not ordain its first female until 1996 when Revd Angela Morgan was chosen, and did not have its first female president until 2018 when they elected Revd Karen Kirlew. Many females in Jamaica are often subjected to regulations and cultural practices which prevent them from realizing their full God-given potential as human beings, and as such have many more glass ceilings to break than our men do. Preachers need to appreciate the condition of women and intentionally uplift them as beings made in the image of God and equal to men.

Jamaican preachers operate in a different environment than their

US counterparts, for instance, who operate under the principle of the separation of Church and State; or their UK counterparts for whom there is a state church, the Anglican Church, which has certain rights and privileges over other denominations. Then there are those in Jamaica who want the church to avoid involvement in the affairs of the country and concentrate on "saving the souls" only. However, Jamaican preachers should see themselves as part of the national development process.

In addition to a knowledge of the local heritage and history, the Jamaican preacher needs an understanding of global trends – the thinking behind a new definition of gender which is now determined by the idea of "who I feel I want to be"; a common belief that one should not be restricted in sharing erotic love with whomever; the position that certain criticisms, though not libellous, can be classified as hate speech. The compassionate preacher will appreciate and be conversant with a different point of view, even while maintaining his or her settled position based on an interpretation of scripture.

PREACHING AS A PERSONAL CALL

Ultimately, it is Jesus who calls and commissions preachers who have had a personal experience of His grace and mercy. Preaching is partially a personal testimony by the preacher about the relationship between God and the preacher, what the preacher hears from God, and what the preacher experiences with God and wants to share with others for the honour of God. Every preacher is following in the tradition of Jesus, the supreme preacher. Preaching is a faithful continuation of the ministry of Jesus, in the name of and by the power of Christ who embodies the word of God in his words and deeds. Jesus calls and commissions preachers to be like him and to liberate the people:

> Di Spirit a di Laad de pan mi,
> kaaz im pik mi out
> fi kyari gud nyuuz go gi puo piipl.
> Im sen mi fi mek di prizna dem nuo se dem ago frii,
> fi mek blain piipl nuo se dem a-go si agen,
> fi mek piipl we a sofa nuo se dem naa go sofa fi eva.
> An im pik mi out fi mek piipl nuo se dis a di taim wen di Laad a-go siev im piipl dem.
> (Luuk 4:18-19)

Introduction

As a Jamaican preacher, my style is mainly as an expositor of a biblical text. By and large, the sermons progress sequentially with argumentation and reasonable points, and conclude with specific applications. I usually state the problem and what is the issue at hand; then, a remedy to deal with the problem is offered in God as revealed in Jesus and inspired by the Holy Spirit. Then, finally, the consequences of making a biblical decision are given.

In this work, I am documenting a sample of what the congregation at Boulevard Baptist heard weekly for thirty years. Hopefully, after reading these sermons, you will be better able to know what to do and what not to do, based on the mistakes I have made.

The focus of these sermons is not on the syntax, semantics or stylistics of preaching. The focus is on content, biblical interpretation and relevance to context and enduring meaning. Relevance to context means speaking the truth in relation to the real, at the moment of the need of the congregation; it is not a matter of telling people what they want to hear. The sermons were edited to get rid of most of the fluff which was appropriate for delivery, but not for reading, and factual errors were corrected. In addition, I ensured proper identification of people mentioned in the script. Please note that I used some poetic licence in these sermons. There are times when they departed from the conventional rules of language to create an intended effect. Some things in the script might have been omitted inadvertently during delivery, and some words that were delivered might have been said on the spur of the moment, and hence are not in the script.

These sermons were divided into four chapters and an epilogue. The first chapter contains six sermons preached during the COVID-19 pandemic, while the second chapter contains three sermons delivered at three sessions of the annual Jamaica Baptist Union General Assembly when I was president of the JBU (2016-18). There is a debate on whether what the president of the JBU preaches during the opening service of a JBU assembly is a sermon or a presidential address. By address, I mean that the president would "address" national, regional and international socioeconomic and political issues, usually at the beginning of the presentation. However, based on my understanding of a sermon, when I speak, I also consider such issues from the perspective of the Bible, and then announce the demands of God in light of his goodness, graciousness and greatness. Therefore, I am sitting on the fence by calling them "presidential proclamations", and in so doing, I hope to appease those who call them presidential addresses and those who think that they should be presidential sermons. The first sermon asserts that Jesus, through his death and resurrection, has called us to be Living in Partnership, and to build on this foundation we need to practise humility, value dignity, maintain civility and embrace community, based on a belief in the equality of all human beings which must be grounded in the reality that every human being was made in the image of God. The second sermon affirms that our raison d'être is to engage in "witnessing fervently". We are stewards of the same mission Jesus engaged in. Our life's purpose is to pursue God's mission in the world. The third one, "Giving Freely" advocates that giving is not merely giving tithes and offering, but offering the total self sacrificially to be at the disposal of God whenever He chooses and wherever He chooses to send us.

Then chapter three has five sermons preached on special occasions, one of which was a sermon preached at the ordination service for Revd Derrick Saddler, son of Boulevard Baptist and pastor of Stokes Hall Circuit of Baptist churches, entitled "Neutral on Nothing", which was a call to be on the side of those who are left out and left behind. Then, on the 55th anniversary of the Jamaica Teachers' Association (JTA), the sermon was a call for the congregation to do what is right by acting justly, loving mercy and walking humbly with God. A sermon that encouraged the drinking of wine only to the amount that is optimum for the human body to perform at its best in doing God's work, on the occasion of a beer company celebrating 100 years, spurred some controversy. One preached on the 50th anniversary of the JTA Co-op Credit Union encouraged people to "Eat with Sinners", following the example, mission and mandate of Jesus to extend friendship and fellowship to the people who are the outcasts of society. The fifth one entitled "Celebration" was preached at the 1989 JBU Assembly when I was pastor of the Fletcher's Grove/Mt Pelier Circuit of Baptist churches. It proclaimed that our primary focus in life is to praise God in eating, drinking or whatever we are doing.

Chapter four contains six sermons preached at funerals for founding pastor of Boulevard Baptist; two deacons of Boulevard Baptist; the oldest person in the world; a teenager and a child, the latter two connected to Boulevard Baptist. One well-known preacher in a dismissive tone classifies the last sermon as a eulogy. However, my funeral sermons remind the congregants of their mortality and the hope of life after death through the resurrection of Jesus. There is an

Figure 1. Devon Dick, Pastor (with face shield as protection against the COVID-19 virus), Boulevard Baptist Church

Photograph by Marva Lambert, member, Boulevard Baptist (10 September 2020)

interpretation of the scriptures in light of the life of the deceased and how the good qualities of the deceased relate to that biblical text. Further, there is a call to a right relationship with God, and to live well with all in order to experience a meaningful life.

Finally, the epilogue contains an evangelistic sermon calling people to repentance toward God and to faith in our Lord Jesus, the Christ.

ONE: PREACHING DURING A PANDEMIC

Take Loving to Another Level

> **Scripture Lesson: John 13:34-35**
> *"A new commandment I give to you, that you love one another: just as I have loved you"* (John 13:34 ESV).

» *9 August 2020*

Jesus exhorted his disciples to take loving to another level, to increase the intensity of their love. The significance of taking loving to higher heights and deeper depths was underscored by the new commandment "love one another as I have loved you" (NIV) being mentioned three times within three chapters of John, from chapter 13 to chapter 15. Furthermore, this new commandment "love one another as I have loved you" was part of the last words and last wish of Jesus in his farewell discourse to the disciples. The last words of Jesus before his death are very substantial and special.

So, what was so special and significant about this new commandment, "love one another as I have loved you"? What was so novel about this commandment, this injunction? What was fresh, first and far-reaching about this commandment, this ordinance? I will offer seven features of this new commandment.

One, it was a new commandment because it had never been issued or used before. It was "hot off the press". It was newly minted, brand new.

ONE • Preaching during a Pandemic

Two, this commandment was new because it was not in the Ten Commandments or any other law. In fact, it was not even in the two greatest commandments.

Three, this new commandment will never grow old. It will never be obsolete, never stale, never useless and has no expiry date.

Four, this new commandment will never be replaced, or improved on, or superseded.

Five, it did not exclude other moral precepts, but rather included all other moral codes and precepts.

Six, love was not based on Jewish status and limited to loving family, friends, fellow citizens, and our favourite people only. This love cannot be confined to one's race, nationality or ethnicity.

Seven, and last, the commandment was new and different, in that Jesus was the standard: "as I have loved you". Jesus' own act of love was to be a model and motivation for his disciples. His life was a model and example of how to love, such as when Jesus washed the feet of his disciples. It was a call to express the same type and degree of love that they experienced from Jesus. This type of love was generated specifically through faith in Jesus. This love was facilitated because they belonged to Christ. This new commandment has a peculiarly Christian character. The novelty lies in the new motive, which is the love of Christ – a new moral absolute based on Jesus.

What was new about this commandment? It was based on Jesus' standard, not Jewish standards; it was singular and unique; it could not be superseded; it will never become stale; and it is all-encompassing.

This newness and novelty were in keeping with the character of Jesus who challenged the disciples to take loving to another level. For example, Jesus said, "You have heard it said, 'Love your neighbor and hate your enemy'; **but I** tell you love your enemies" (Matt. 5:43-44 NIV). Jesus was quoting rabbinic teaching, but he broke with that interpretation of the Mosaic law and gave his own interpretation as the new Rabbi. Jesus articulated: do not love your fellow citizens only, while hating foreigners and perceiving them as enemies. Formerly, the children of God hated the Canaanites and Amalekites and destroyed them. However, Jesus said "love your enemies; love those who are antagonistic to you, who persecute you and who say all manner of evil about you." Wish them well. Therefore, Jesus took loving to another level by stating that we should love our enemies.

Also, "loving one another as Jesus loved us" was higher than "love your neighbour as yourself", because what if we do not love ourselves? It would mean we are going to love our neighbours in the same way. Indeed, some people hate themselves; they have poor self-esteem and poor self-worth. So, they are incapable of loving others properly and adequately. They are incapable of loving others because they do not love themselves.

And even when we have a healthy human love of self, that is still an offering far too small, way too inadequate and far below the standard to be compared with the divine, unconditional and sacrificial love of Jesus.

So, Jesus took loving to the highest level when he said "love one another as I have loved you". And how did Jesus love? Jesus loved unconditionally; he took the initiative and he forgave all. He gave all, and he gave his best to all.

LOVE LIKE THE ALMIGHTY

God loves deeply and unconditionally whether or not we return his love. God loves people who are undeserving, unworthy, ungrateful and ungodly.

God's love is sacrificial, in that Christ gave his life for all humans. And in return we must emulate that example of being willing to make the ultimate sacrifice and offer our lives for others. That is not too hard; that is not demanding too much. Members of the security forces give up their lives for persons who are uncouth and unkind. Also, first responders such as firemen, doctors and nurses interact with COVID-19 patients and risk their lives for people they do not even know. Furthermore, every husband must love his wife "as Christ loved the church and gave himself up for her" (Eph. 5:25 NIV). Every husband worth his salt must be willing to die for his wife. So, if husbands can give up their lives for their wives, if the police can do it and first responders, then with the help of the Holy Spirit, we can also love like that. We can love like the Almighty God, being willing to give up our lives.

LOVE ALL

God has made all human beings to give love. All can love. All are capable of loving, and that includes you. Not all can love erotically or sexually for various reasons. However, all who belong to Christ can love each other as Christ loved the Church. Everybody can express divine love unconditionally, wishing the other the very best and having the highest regard for the other. So, then, perhaps when we see members not loving like Christ loved the Church, it could be that they are not part of the family of God, and might end up worse than Judas.

Judas' love was self-centred, in that he wanted a political solution so that he could be part of the ruling political class and lord it over others. What type of love we are displaying?

We are called to love all, including the young members of criminal gangs. We are to love especially the widows, the orphans, the foreigners, the strangers and the poor (Zech. 7:9-10) who need a practical demonstration of love. It is a call to serve all. Love all, and build a future of hope by loving all as Christ loved the church.

Conclusion

Do you want to take loving to another level? Heed the words of Jesus to love one another as he did. When we love one another as Christ loved us, then others will know that we are Christians by our love.
Amen.

I Am a Jamaican Christian

Scripture Lesson: 2 Corinthians 11

"I do not think I am in the least inferior to those 'super-apostles'" (2 Cor. 11:5 NIV).

» *2 August 2020*

Jamaicans are known for being "tallawah" – punching above our weight, having an impact greater than our size would indicate. Jamaica is the proverbial "small axe [that] fall big tree". So, through our music, athletics, language and cuisine, we have had a wider reach, a more lasting impact and greater influence than our size would dictate. We Jamaicans are not culturally inferior to people from other countries with longer histories, more people and greater resources.

Similarly, Paul in 2 Corinthians 11 explains that he was not inferior to the so-called super-apostles, these "overmuch" apostles. He acknowledged that he was not a trained orator (6) as apparently some of the celebrity apostles were. He was not as charismatic as those overbearing apostles. His appearance was not striking. However, he had knowledge and was able to read the Old Testament in the original language. His long and hard labour for the Lord could stand up to scrutiny and compare favourably to these "nuff" and "extra" apostles. Paul was not going to genuflect and salute these "fly-by-night", "hurry come up", so-called super-apostles. In fact, Paul was bold and held back no punches when he shamed these false apostles who were preaching another gospel to these gullible Corinthians.

But the million-dollar question is: are Jamaican Christians inferior to Christians elsewhere? What are or should be the features and identity of a Jamaican Christian? If the Jamaican Christian can say truthfully "I am Black" and "I am bold", then he or she is not inferior to any so-called super-apostle coming from "foreign".

I Am Black

Some of you might be uncomfortable to say "I am Black". But why? People can say "I am European" and "I am Asian", but people of African descent are afraid to say "I am Black". This is demonstrated by some Black people being uneasy saying "Black Lives Matter". However, does the claim that "Black Lives Matter" mean that the lives of other races are not important? No. It is claimed that other races are treated as if only their lives matter, and only they are chosen by God. "Black Lives Matter" is a statement based on data and evidence that Black lives are treated as inferior, as subject to oppression, when compared to how Whites and lighter-skinned people are treated.

"I am Black" is also affirming that it is God who created us differently and created different races. It is a way of saying that Black lives are also made in the image of God and should be treated equally, fairly, and with equity. Blacks are not inferior to other races.

Paul claimed "I am a Jew" (22). He was a Hebrew who spoke Aramaic and was able to read the Law and the Prophets in the original Aramaic. Paul a "Hebrew of Hebrews" (Phil. 3:5) was affirming his nationality and ethnicity. Paul's parents were Jews of Palestine, and while his place of birth was in Tarsus, he was not a Greek Jew and he was no Gentile. We are Gentiles and we are Black. Saying "I am Black" is not creating divisions, just as Paul saying he is an orthodox Jew was not creating division between Jews and Gentiles.

ONE ● Preaching during a Pandemic

Unfortunately, most Jamaican Black men want a wife who will put "a little milk in his coffee" when children are born. Recently, a senior member of parliament told me that, from childhood, he knew he did not want his children to come out Black because of the abuse and mistreatment he encountered in Jamaica because he was a Black man. Some of us, when we were growing up, our mothers pinched our noses so that our noses could be straight and look more European, and we remember girls straightening their hair to look European. This is self-hatred. This is despising what God has made in his image. Credit is due to national hero Marcus Garvey and former Prime Minister Michael Manley for encouraging Black pride and promoting all things African. So, there is no shame in saying "I am Black".

Furthermore, to proudly say "I am Black" is to recognize and affirm the role of Africa in the Bible. On Friday, Revd Dr George Mulrain, Methodist minister, said at the Gregory Park Baptist emancipation lecture, "The Bible is filled with references to Africa. The biblical world view is distinctly African." Simon, who carried our Lord's cross, was from North Africa. The Apostle Mark was a Black apostle. Jesus spent time in Egypt, which is North Africa. Moses was in Egypt. Did not Solomon talk about being "Black and beautiful" (Song of Songs 1:5 NASB). Guess how many times Ethiopia is mentioned in the Bible. There are twenty references to Ethiopia in the Bible: 19 in the Old Testament (Genesis, Esther, Job, 2 in the Psalms, 6 in Isaiah, 4 in Ezekiel) and one in the New (Acts 8). Philip baptized an Ethiopian eunuch, who went and spread the gospel in Ethiopia.

One of the names George Liele (the man who started Baptist work in Jamaica in 1783) called his congregants was the "Ethiopian Baptists". However, nowadays Baptists would never want to associate with being called Ethiopian Baptists, but would rather identify and associate with European Baptists, the same Baptists who will not read a resolution on reparations at their global meetings. However, to be Black is not to be inferior. We are co-workers and coequals with every Christian of any race.

One of the main findings of my book *The Cross and the Machete* (2009) was that Christianity grew in Jamaica in the 18th and 19th centuries due to the work and witness of Black Jamaicans rather than foreign missionaries. In addition, national heroes and Baptist pastors Sam Sharpe, Paul Bogle and George William Gordon were not inferior interpreters of the Bible when compared to the English missionaries.

They understood God and interpreted scriptures differently, claiming that God was interested and involved in their struggle for fairness.

Be comfortable in your own skin. Be relaxed in the way you present yourselves and interact with others, which will display that you have a clear understanding of your own abilities and of the situation. "I am Black" is affirming that we are not inferior or superior to anyone.

I AM BOLD

There was a movie released in 2016 called "I am Bolt". The name meant that Jamaican superstar Usain Bolt was the best sprinter the world has ever seen. There was also another 2016 movie, "I am Wrath", starring John Travolta whose character found purpose in life by seeking revenge and killing the gang members responsible for his wife's murder.

A Black Jamaican Christian saying that "I am bold" is not making a claim of being the best or announcing an intent to embark on a mission of revenge. Rather, it is a brave statement that we will be fearless in facing the difficulties and dangers while being fair at all times to all people, especially those who are vulnerable and poor.

FEARLESSNESS

US Congressman John Lewis died at 80 years old, and was buried last week. At age 26, he was the youngest speaker at the "I have a Dream" march on Washington in 1963. He was beaten by Whites and his skull was cracked, yet this ordained Baptist minister still preached non-violence. Furthermore, he spoke truth to power in the US Congress and was said to cause "good trouble". He was fearless. We also need to be fearless and cause "good trouble" and "necessary trouble".

Sometimes, preachers have to fearlessly identify the false "over-much" apostles. Some of these false apostles enjoy some success; they might even create some miracles and do some good. But these celebrity apostles are like "a gangster don" doing good, or like a corrupt politician doing some good. These false apostles emphasize their entitlement to financial gifts from the Believers. Furthermore, these "nuff" and "boasy" apostles are usually flamboyant, gaudy "gold diggers". They have no track record of service and have not left any body of work to be judged. They teach that prayer is mainly about getting material things for self-centred enjoyment. Most of their prophecies do not come true and they claim we can all be rich and healthy, which is not possible. They are ministers of Satan.

We need people who will stand up to our abusers, manipulators, control freaks, sexual freaks and mental health destroying parasites. The late Deacon Maud Daley, whose funeral service was held on Friday, was politically active, and had fearlessly lain in the road in a political protest for justice for workers. We need a fearless Christian community known for creating a just society. Oh, for more Christians in Jamaica, the Caribbean and across the world who would be fearless; fearing no one and nothing, whether things seen or unseen; fearless in spite of the threat of death; fearless in the face of principalities and powers; fearless in the face of things present or things to come. Say "I am bold", so I fear no one and nothing.

Fairness

We must be fearless, and we must also be fair, even-handed and just. We must be bold and committed to creating a fair and just society in Jamaica. That is the mandate for all Jamaican Christians, to use their collective voices, resources and platforms to effect sustainable and just change in society, thereby allowing God's will to be done "on earth as it is in heaven". Sometimes Christians might even engage in protests and marches to help create a fair society based on justice.

Christians must not only criticize the unfairness, corruption, classism and colourism in our society, but must also deliberately engage in appropriate action in order to create a holy nation. Do not just pass the beaten-up and bleeding "Samaritan", but stop and help. Get involved. Get your hands dirty. Yes, we listen and we lament, but we must agitate for legislative changes so that every Jamaican may account for unexplained wealth and the Integrity Commission can help to prevent corruption. Baptist churches can unite around legislation for criminal justice reform, transparency in government board selection, and a court system that is accessible, affordable and easily available. The church collective needs to engage in advocacy and activism for better governance by cabinet ministers, more fair and just policies, and a less violent political culture. God calls us to be politically engaged while rooted in the gospel of Jesus, the Christ crucified.

When the Baptist missionaries came to Jamaica they were told not to interfere with the socioeconomic conditions of the enslaved, but just to preach to their souls and ignore the slums they lived in. And today, some say just preach and change their hearts and leave the nation alone. However, the people of God must collectively work toward a more fair and just society.

From the beginning of scripture, we see God redeeming not isolated individuals, but reforming a whole people into a godly society, "a kingdom of priests and a holy nation" (Exod. 19:6 NIV; 1 Pet. 2:9 NIV). The Jews were led through the wilderness, not as individuals but as a nation to be an example to other nations. Christians are therefore called upon to be an example by creating a culture of social justice for persons who are poor and weak. There needs to be more equitable use of land and resources, especially for the thousands who are in unplanned communities. The Church must loosen the chains of injustice (Isa. 58:6-7). God calls his people to actively break systems of oppression and create a fair and just Jamaica.

In the New Testament, the Church in Acts 2 strove to obey by committing to prayer, education, the equitable distribution of resources, and the provision of housing, clothing and food to those in need, especially the widows. We must be a community of justice, and this means having a concern for the poor and working towards fair systems and equitable policies for all.

Christians ought to be involved in politics and be interested in how the resources of God are handled, and whether people who are poor have access to opportunities and resources. Take for example the Auditor General's report on the Jamaica Urban Transit Company (JUTC), which unearthed that the managing director only has a high school diploma when the job requires a postgraduate certification. The board's reaction is that all such persons have to enrol in a university by September. What if the university rejects those persons? And even if successful, the company would have to wait five years for the person to become qualified. Up until recently, people with qualifications have not been able to find jobs, including 103 doctors. Furthermore, do not blame the managing director and others, but rather blame the board members who employed them without due regard. Concentrate on the enablers of corruption and be fair to qualified persons seeking employment.

ONE ● Preaching during a Pandemic

Conclusion

A frog decided to jump to the top of a tree ten feet tall. All the other frogs shouted, "It is impossible." Still the frog jumped to the top. How did he do it when others said he could not jump so high? Because he was deaf, and when he saw their mouths moving, he thought everyone was encouraging him to reach to the top. Do not listen to the naysayers. Just jump and pledge to be bold, based on your identity as a Black Jamaican Christian.

Listen for the Voice of God

> **Scripture Lesson: Psalm 1**
> *"And he shall be like a tree planted by the rivers of water, that bringeth forth fruit… and whatsoever he doeth shall prosper"*
> *(Ps. 1:3 KJV).*

» 26 July 2020

On Tuesday, a US televangelist, of the network Inspirational Ministries, told his followers that nothing moves in heaven until something moves on earth. In other words, God has to be spurred into action by our deeds – in this instance, planting a seed offering of US$1,000 in his ministry with an expected hundredfold increase within 90 days. The US televangelist said that, "As soon as you pick up the phone to make the contribution of $1,000, the blessing, increase and prosperity will be yours." But is his statement true, that God acts when we give money to someone's ministry? I do not think so.

This thinking and position come from an age-old practice. In the 11th century, Roman Catholics paid indulgences (money) to escape punishment in the afterlife. An indulgence is the means by which a sinner can gain a full or partial remission of temporal punishment for sins after the sinner confesses and receives absolution. German preacher, John Tetzel, Dominican indulgence vendor, famously said, "As soon as the coin in the coffer rings, the soul from purgatory springs" (Wikipedia). Some say "Jamaica moves" because of money, and others say "God moves" because of money. What an audacity to belittle God and his ways.

These persons, their thinking and their utterances are making God into a material God. They have made God in their image, a sort of golden calf god. Are those the false teachings we are following? What is our main source of advice, information and wisdom? Who informs our choices? What shapes our values and attitudes? Who is whispering in our ears? A piece of advice to us all: avoid listening to the ungodly, avoid taking advice from the sinners and avoid taking instructions from the scornful. These are the three types of wicked people to avoid and stay far from. And each type is worse than the last. Avoid, one, the ungodly; sidestep, two, sinners; and shun, three, the scornful. Do not be one with them, that is, do not have fellowship with the ungodly, the sinners and the scornful.

Why avoid the ungodly? Because the ungodly are persons who are restless, lacking in self-control, led by worldly desires and passions and they encourage mischief. Why sidestep the sinners? Because they are wrongdoers; they are given to a life of crime; they are serial scammers and constant crooks. And finally, why do we shun the worst ones, the scornful, the mockers. They are rebellious. They fly in the face of God. They make fun of what is good and holy. Avoid these evildoers, and their patron the Evil One, and his evil system. Have nothing to do with them and live a blessed and happy life. Happy is the one who does not throw his lot in with, or his weight behind the wicked or participate in their plans, projects and proposals. Happy is the man who does not take part in their actions, who does not follow the same moral paths. Happy is the man who does not have fellowship and is not in oneness with those who mock God, mock God's word and mock God's people.

To put it positively: If you want to live a blessed and happy life, then the word is this – delight in the word of God, meditate on it day and night and heed the voice of God. According to Psalm 1, if you want to flourish and be fruitful, if you want to have influence and an impact, then listen for the voice of God.

Avoid Bad Counsel

"Blessed is the man that walketh not in the counsel of the ungodly" (Ps. 1:1 KJV). Beware of bad advice from wicked people, those who are enablers of corruption. Do not dwell on bad advice, nor think it

ONE ● PREACHING DURING A PANDEMIC

over. Do not settle on it, nor sit on the proposal. Do not "par" with the scornful, do not hold long conversations with the ungodly, and keep your physical distance from those who mock God. When you are invited out to discuss evil with sinners, the word is "tan a yuh yard". When people come with some "chickeenery" business and some "Jim Screechie" underhand dealings, "cry excuse" and walk away from them. Do not sleep with them; do not embrace them; do not owe them money; do not lend them money. Have nothing to do with <u>them</u>. When we deliberately associate with those who openly mock God it means we "tun back" or backslide.

Some people like to push the envelope and believe that they can embrace and become entangled with the ungodly, the sinners and the scornful and still avoid being influenced by their bad advice. Wrong. Sometimes we feel we are wise enough to pick sense out of nonsense. Wrong. We are modern and so we may say "let all ideas flourish". Wrong. Satan and his agents are so deceitful that they can deceive the very elect. It is safer just to avoid bad advice given by people who are ungodly, who are sinners, and who are scornful.

- Show me your advisers, and I will tell you who you are.
- Show me your cabinet, and I will tell you who you are.
- Show me your friends on Facebook, and I will tell you whether you are getting bad advice.
- Show me who you are close to and who you hang out with, and I will tell you whether you are on a path of destruction.
- Show me your network of influence, and I will tell you where you are going.

Friends, if bad advice goes into our being, then bad actions follow. What bad advice did we receive early in life, and followed, and how did it mess up our heads? Last week, I read about a pastor who wrote the seventeen worst pieces of advice given to him by older pastors. What about us? What are the worst pieces of advice we ever received? Those who are worshipping with us via live streaming, please go to the chat room and write down the worse pieces of advice given to you, whether about career, relationships or family life, so that others will know it is bad advice to be avoided.

Let Booker T. Washington (1856-1915), Black American educator, orator and author, inspire us with these words: "Associate yourself with people of good quality..." (Wikipedia). Good advice. Those watching on live streaming, please go to the chat room and write down the best advice you received in your Christian walk, or in your career, or in marriage. Associate yourself with people of good quality who will give you good advice. What is the good advice? Delight in the law of God; delight in the word; and delight in scriptures.

DELIGHT CONSTANTLY IN THE BIBLE (PS. 1:2)

To listen for the voice of God we have to constantly search the scriptures. We need the word of God. The word of God is important and vital to life. Therefore, study to show thyself approved. Do not select scripture passages to support our ungodly lifestyles, or to support our political ideologies, or to support the behaviour of our favourite public figure. But read the word of God for edification.

<u>Meditate</u> on the word daily. Not just one verse here and there, or even a chapter, but read the whole book whenever possible. Think hard on it. Sleep on it. Joshua <u>meditated</u> on the Book of Law. When David was overwhelmed, he meditated on the word of God (Ps. 143). Deliberately think about the word of God and remember what he has done in the past and what he promises to do.

As we study God's word, we will be guided in how to organize our resources and relationships. We will share God's resources for optimal ministry, and promote the wellness of humanity. Systems will be so organized as not to encourage greed but equity, with persons getting what is needed for optimal living, witness and loving.

OBEY GOD'S VOICE

Some mistakenly believe that just diligently searching the scriptures and hearing the voice of God but then doing nothing is okay. These people are consumers of the worship experience only. They come to church and listen, and then they go home and listen to more religious programmes. And now they also join Bible study meetings on Zoom, and that is it. They enjoy worship as if it were entertainment – a spectator sport – rather than expecting to be a participant. How do we participate? We heed the voice of God and do what he commands.

How about church leaders? Are we willing to risk our lives as we pray for the sick? Will church leaders retreat and forsake the assembling together of the brethren, and forfeit the opportunity to get to know each other better? Getting to know each other better can lead

ONE ● PREACHING DURING A PANDEMIC

to identifying strengths for carrying out God's ministry. Furthermore, knowing each other better helps us to overcome prejudices and work out misunderstandings. Remember, God promises to be present in a special and significant way when two or three are gathered together in his name for his cause, to confess to him, to honour his authority and power, and to make the place where they are a place of prayer, praise, petition and preaching. Whenever there are two or three, there is a church. The strength of a church is not measured by numbers but by nature, that is, the fulfillment of her mandate and reason for being. It is about oneness and communion with God. It is about God confirming and approving decisions made by the church members. In the smallest gathering, as a church, Jesus is there, by his Spirit, to impart himself to them.

When we obey God, then we become a new creation. We will experience a reversal of the moral decline in our lives. We will shun corruption, crime and confusion. When we obey God, then we will respect life, respect all of life, respect law and order and destroy pagan worship centres. Then we will be happy.

This morning, I will speak about one area of human agency God uses to speak, that is through his messengers. In Deuteronomy 18, God told the Israelites that he will speak through his servants, the prophets. Therefore, obey the true prophet. But how will you know a genuine prophet? According to verse 22 of the same chapter, "If what a prophet proclaims in the name of the Lord does not take place or come true, that is a message the Lord has not spoken" (NIV). Yesterday, I heard a man on a religious radio station praying and saying and telling God that "a storm" will not affect Jamaica destructively, but that rain will come to fill up the dam. Is he a true prophet? Let us see whether these prophecies in prayer will come true. There is also that televangelist who promised that if you give him US$1,000, in 90 days it will increase a hundredfold; let us see if it comes through for everybody. A true prophet's predictions are accurate and correct. What he or she says comes true. What is said is validated and his or her position on an issue is vindicated. In time, the prophet's position is justified and held to be true. The true prophet will encourage people to stay in the narrow way, and to be loyal and faithful to God as revealed in Jesus and empowered by the Holy Spirit. Follow the teachings of a true prophet and it will result in you being your best self, your ideal, noble self.

When we look back, we realize that US Baptist Pastor Martin Luther King, Jr was a true prophet. Baptist Pastors Sam Sharpe, Paul Bogle and George William Gordon were also true prophets, because they were on the right side of history, and their words have come to pass. In addition, true prophets display moral courage to speak truth whatever the cost. True prophets want to see people prosper and flourish.

What is God's voice saying to us? António Guterres, UN secretary-general, speaking at the 18th Nelson Mandela Annual Lecture, said that the pandemic was like an x-ray on society, exposing the underbelly of inequalities and discrimination. He claimed that the pandemic would trigger famines and push 100 million more people into poverty. Is God speaking to us through the x-ray of coronavirus? God is speaking and we need to obey. Do whatever God says.

Conclusion

Two roads are before you. This is the worldview and philosophy of the Psalms, the Old Testament and New Testament. You are either blessed or cursed; either saved or unsaved; either happy or unhappy; either serving God or serving mammon; either worshipping the Saviour or worshipping Satan. Choose today whom you will serve. Choose today to be blessed. Choose today to be happy. Choose today to avoid the bad counsel of the ungodly sinners and the scornful. Choose today to delight in the word of God. Choose today to listen for the voice of God.

ONE ● Preaching during a Pandemic

USE THE OPPORTUNITIES OF YOUTHFULNESS

Scripture Lesson: Ecclesiastes 12:1, 9-14
"Let us hear the conclusion of the whole matter: Fear God, and keep his commandments: for this is the whole duty of man" (Eccles. 12:13 KJV).

» *19 July 2020*

Last week, Benjamin Presley Keough, grandson of Elvis Presley the "King of Rock and Roll", died at age 27. This famous, rich kid who so resembled his grandfather Elvis Presley died from self-inflicted gunshot wounds. Benjamin had fame, fortune and a loving family. Why would someone who seemingly had so much going for him take his own life? Obviously, Benjamin came to the conclusion that life was wearisome and worrisome, life was futile, frustrating and foolish, and life was boring, meaningless and senseless. For Benjamin, apparently, there was nothing worthwhile to look forward to in life. There was no joy, no hope and no future.

Where can we find answers regarding meaning and purpose in life? Where will joy and celebration be found in this life, and how can we help to make the most of young lives? In these troubling times, what future is there for our young people? Let us turn to the word of God as revealed in Ecclesiastes 12 (NIV). The wise writer of this , of Ecclesiastes realized that one should maximize one's youthful days. He came to this conclusion after reflecting on life experiences. He noticed people growing old with declining strength, wasting away, wrinkled, having lost all outward beauty, suffering dementia, and with sagging skin, trembling hands and wobbling knees. Old men were losing their vim, vigour and vitality. Old age made people feel sad, unhappy, distressed and embarrassed. And saddest of all was to be old before one's time.

So, after mature reflection, this writer gave advice which almost anyone could relate to. The advice he gave was not about doctrines and dogma, and one did not have to come from a Christian home to understand what he was saying. He made common sense, summary statements. They were gems for life. They were practical and pragmatic proverbs in this chapter, such as "all is vanity" (12:8), or "and much study is a weariness of the flesh" (12:12) (some students who have exams might agree), or "remember your Creator in the days of your youth" (12:1).

To understand this book and the aim of the book, you cannot stop at chapter 3, which tells us that "to everything there is a season" (3:1) and that "that which befalleth the sons of men befalleth beasts" (3:19), which is death, and that "all are of the dust, and all turn to dust again" (3:20). If we stop there, we will think that Solomon was depressed and suicidal, because life was meaningless. But one has to read the book to its end, that is, to chapter 12. The penultimate verse of the book reads: "Let us hear the conclusion of the whole matter: Fear God, and keep his commandments: for this is the whole duty of man" (12:13). This verse helps us to understand Solomon and his musings. This verse helps us to interpret the entire book.

The point of this chapter and the entire book is that the purpose of life is to respect and revere God, to love and be loyal to God, to worship and witness for God and the best time to start is now; the best time to start is in the days of our youth. It is not rocket science to realize that one should make best use of the time when we are young, make the best use of the time when we are strongest physically, when we are at the zenith of our intellectual prowess, when our creative juices are flowing.

The book of Ecclesiastes targets young people, including millennials. This book reflects the spirit of this age, the present-day mood of egotism: "There is nothing better than that a man should rejoice in his own works; for that is his portion" (3:22). There is cynicism (futility of life), and there is also realism in the text: "Let us hear the conclusion of the whole matter: Fear God and keep his commandments: for this is the whole duty of man" (12:13 KJV).

So, what is the conclusion of the matter? The concluding chapter tells us how to live a good life in the face of upcoming old age. Two things: remember thy Creator in thy youth and revel in life.

REMEMBER THY CREATOR IN THY YOUTH

> "Remember now thy Creator in the days of thy youth, while the evil days come not, nor the years draw nigh, when thou shalt say, I have no pleasure in them..." (Eccles. 12:1 KJV).

Why is it necessary to remember God while we are young? Remembering is a response to the goodness, greatness and graciousness of

ONE ● PREACHING DURING A PANDEMIC

God to us. God in his goodness offers us pardon and forgiveness for our sins. He justifies us as if we have never sinned. He cleanses us from all unrighteousness. In addition, God is great and provides for us this unique universe and wonderful world to sustain our lives. Furthermore, God is gracious and gives us more than we ask for, more than we deserve, and he offers us what we could not afford to pay for. In your youthful days, remember the goodness, greatness and graciousness of God.

There is also great satisfaction in knowing the thinking and thoughts of God from early. There is no greater joy than being in a right relationship with God from an early age. Grow up with God from the days of your youth, so that his ways will become your ways. The truth is, when adults become Christians late in life and are set in their old ways, old habits and old behaviours, they are often hard to change. But when the tree is bent from early, the results are different. So then, now is the day of salvation. Now is the time to serve God. Give the best days of your life to God.

The rich young man did not remember God in his youth (Matt. 19:16-22). Here was a powerful, wealthy young leader who turned his back on God and had more faith in his wealth than in God. But what shall it profit a young man to gain the whole world and lose his health? What shall it profit a young man to gain the whole world and lose his relationship with God?

Remember thy Creator in the days of your youth because you are **not risk averse**, but willing to take risks. In the days of thy youth is when you are daring. Generally, the older we get, the more conservative we become, with concerns about pension, preservation of life and position in life. Youth can be the time when you have faith in God that can move mountains. At that stage, young people anticipate great things from God and try great things for God. Young people, think big and go hard. Young people, take a risk for God. Young people, launch out into the deep with God.

Young people, the Lord calls you because you are strong (1 John 2:14). Use your strength, but not to bully others and abuse others. Instead, use your God-given strength, power and might to protect the people who are victims and comfort persons who are vulnerable. Use your strong shoulders for grieving people to lean on.

Young people, give the heights of your intellectual powers in the service of God. Scientific research shows that the greatest intellectual development takes place normally in the first nine years of a child's life. Use your intellect in the ministry of God.

You are young and gifted and your creative juices are flowing. Use new and different ideas in the mission of God.

Do you notice that it is mainly young people involved in the Black Lives Matter protests in the USA, UK and elsewhere? Who is the face of climate change in the world? It is 18-year-old Greta Thunberg, Swedish environmental activist. She has crossed swords with US president Donald Trump and she was not intimidated. Who is leading the struggle for girls' education in the Greater Middle East and the Arab world? It is 23-year-old Malala Yousafzai who was shot at age 15 by the Taliban in Pakistan. Malala, at age 17, became the youngest person to win the Nobel Peace Prize for her advocacy role. Two teenage girls have been turning the world upside down against powerful men and a terrorist organization for the preservation of the environment and the cause of educating females. Young people, God is calling you. Just say, yes, Lord, yes.

Young people, it is the relationship with God that develops in your young days that will carry you throughout your entire life. Because from early, if you store the word of God in your hearts, then you will not sin against God. If you build a relationship with God from early, then you will be daring, knowing that "greater is He that is in you than he that is in the world" (1 John 4:4 KJV). And so, young people, do not panic over disease, duppy or death.

From your early days, set your mind on God and when you grow older you will not depart from God. The best time to start to serve God is in thy youth, and then you will grow in God and with God through adulthood, middle age and old age. So, remember God in the days of your youth. Remember God now.

REVEL IN LIFE IN THY YOUTH

Some people are waiting on retirement to enjoy life; waiting on retirement to travel; waiting on retirement to relax. Some men go through midlife crises and try to recapture their youth by dying their grey hairs black to look young, or by shaving off their hair in the hope of shaving off some years. But it is all in vain.

The call to revel in life is not a call to "do it", that is, to engage in sexual immorality. This is not a support of sex with underage girls or sexual intercourse with young boys. The call to revel in life is not an implicit message to commit adultery. In fact, sexual immorality is not a way to enjoy life because the consequences of sexual immorality can be seen in such things as unwanted pregnancies, unwelcome sexually transmitted diseases (STDs) or unwarranted shame and scandal to loved ones. But even if the sexual immorality does not lead to unwanted pregnancy or unwelcome STDs or unwarranted pain to loved ones, it is not right because it is selfish sexual satisfaction and it is a failure to recognize that we are stewards of our bodies and not owners. Our bodies are the residence of the Holy Spirit, the temple of God, so whatever we do with our bodies and in our bodies ought to be in accordance with God's wishes, God's will and God's way. We ought to enjoy sex in the context of a committed, complementary faithful love relationship.

Yesterday, Mary and I were reflecting on advice we got in 1997, from the late Emma Hutchinson when the church was on a pilgrimage to the Holy Land. She told us to enjoy ourselves. It was sound advice that helped us. I am passing on a similar piece of advice to you: Enjoy life in your youth. Let your youthful days count.

Revelling is to have fun, to gain pleasure from godly living. Which app is the most popular in the world? It is not Facebook or Instagram or Zoom but TikTok. Why? I believe it is because it is a fun app. People want to have fun in this sometimes dreary world. People want to laugh. Everybody wants something to put a smile on his or her face. Enjoy life in the days of your youth. And as the Heptones, a reggae singing group said, "We've got to live some life / Before we're old" (1968 "Party Time").

Learn to do the simple things of life right from the beginning, and there will be no need to lie to cover our tracks, no need to be always looking behind us. Had the politicians who are getting themselves into trouble imbibed certain godly principles from they were young, then certain forms of corruption, crime and scandal might not have become their way of life. When certain philosophies are ingrained in us when we are young, like honesty, for example, then we cannot "thief" other people's money when we are older. Do the simple things right from early, such as speaking the truth, cost it what it will; being honest in our transactions; being loyal and faithful in our relationships; and being dependable in keeping our promises.

Enjoy the fellowship. On Friday, a well-known church leader said there is no need to go to church anymore, because he enjoys the service online, he pays his tithes online, and he does not need any fellowship. However, we are called into fellowship with the triune God (1 Cor. 1:9-10) and with one another. Those who believe in the gospel are united in the Spirit through the Son to the Father. The fellowship of believers has as its model, goal and nature the fellowship that is within the triune God. In the triune God, they are together in everything; they cooperate, they consult and they coordinate. The experience of Christian fellowship exists because the Father through the Son and by the Holy Spirit has established a relationship with human beings.

So, fellowship is not about eating and drinking together only. Fellowship cannot be confined to shaking hands and hugging. Fellowship is not a "vibe", or the feeling that worship service was sweet. Fellowship is a divine calling and activity. It is to partake of the divine nature of God. Fellowship has to do with being "in Christ". Because it is "in Christ", then there is interrelatedness and interdependence among fellow Christians. This interrelatedness, interdependence, relationship, unity, connectivity and communion is fellowship. We need each other to be the best we can be. Fellowship is opposed to social distancing. Fellowship is intimate. Fellowship involves mutual obligation. It is a generous sharing rather than a selfish grabbing. It is a closeness; it is one for all and all for one: "Rejoice with those who rejoice; mourn with those who mourn" (Rom. 12:15 NIV). The good we work for and wish for ourselves is what we should work for and wish for others. That is sweet fellowship.

CONCLUSION

Young people, there are two roads before you. Will you follow the route of Benjamin Presley, who gave up on life and gave up his life? Or will you remember thy Creator in thy youth and respond in repentance to God's goodness, greatness and graciousness? The conclusion of the matter is this: remember God in the time of your youth. Worship, witness and work for God now. Decide for God now. Today is the day of salvation.

ONE ● Preaching during a Pandemic

Start a Moral Revolution

> Scripture Lesson: Mark 6:14-44
> *"You give them something to eat." (Mark 6:37 NIV)*

» 12 July 2020

In Wednesday's edition of the daily newspaper *The Star*, there was a report entitled "Food Now on Hire Purchase". One of our leading furniture stores now offers food on hire purchase to Jamaicans who are low on cash. Since May, customers can credit food baskets which cost as little as J$3,000. The food items on hire purchase include "tin" mackerel, sardines, flour, rice, powdered milk and vegetable oil. Those who acquire food on hire purchase are given 12 weeks to repay at the same interest rate as other furniture items.

The fact that food is on hire purchase is indicative that, for some Jamaicans, scarcity of food is real. Since the outbreak of COVID-19 in Jamaica, more stories are revealed of people living in horrendous conditions and lacking adequate food. Going forward, hunger is likely to get worse because in the last quarter before coronavirus reached Jamaica, that is, the December 2019 quarter, the country recorded a negative growth rate of -0.1 per cent. And the downward trend continues. In the USA, people in cars form long lines to get free food. And there are 12 hot spots in the world, including Venezuela, where starvation is a reality with 12,000 people expected to die weekly. Hunger is real!

But what should be done and not done? The passage from Mark 6:14-44 can give us some insights on how to tackle this basic need for food. In the New Testament, the issue of providing food for hungry people is given prime time. It is therefore not surprising that the only miracle, apart from the resurrection of Jesus, that is recorded in all four gospels of Matthew, Mark, Luke and John is the feeding of the five thousand. Why? Because providing food for people who are hungry is crucial.

Therefore, this feeding of the five thousand was a significant gospel story not to be missed by a people struggling with starvation. Hunger was a major problem in the Roman Empire, so much so that Jesus fed five thousand here, and at another time he fed four thousand, this time with seven loaves and a fish (Matt. 15:32-39 & Mark 8:1-9).

Hunger was a substantial matter, as according to John 6:26 many people were following Jesus for free food and a "bellyful". Most were not interested in becoming disciples. They were just hungry people. And some were so grateful to Jesus for satisfying their hunger, that they wanted to make him king of the Jews (John 6:14). Jesus was feeding the hungry people, and they were thankful to him for giving priority to the provision of food.

Furthermore, the Lord's Prayer, designed and taught by Jesus, highlighted daily bread. The prominence given to daily bread is indicative of the importance of this basic necessity for life.

Additionally, the alleviation of starvation was so important that feeding hungry people was a criterion Jesus gave for entering heaven! One could be forgiven for thinking that church attendance, giving tithes, missionary work, or teaching a Sunday school class would be the benchmarks against which we would be judged in our quest to get into heaven. But alas, Jesus said, "Come, you who are blessed by my Father, take your inheritance, the kingdom prepared for you since the creation of the world. For I was hungry and you gave me something to eat…" (Matt. 25:34-35 NIV). Is it possible that we are missing the significance Jesus attached to feeding hungry people?

One last indicator about the importance of feeding hungry people comes from Mark 6. The disciples collected twelve baskets full of crumbs and scraps: the leftovers from the fish and the bread. Who collects the leftovers, the crumbs and the scraps? Who is it that cannot afford for anything to go to waste? It is people who are poor, hungry and starving. The provision of food was central to the mission of Jesus.

In the Old Testament, the children of God knew famine, and also had to be fed manna daily in the desert. And throughout the New Testament, food for hungry people was an issue. Jesus fed crowds of more than 5,000 and 4,000; people followed Jesus for food; and so desperate were the people for food that not even the crumbs could be wasted. Disciples prayed for daily bread and feeding hungry people will determine our eternal destiny. Providing food for people was of paramount importance to Jesus.

And view the contrast of excess food and drink at Herod's banquet. Of all the gospel writers, Mark provides more details about Herod's banquet and its opulence and decadence. Both Mark and Matthew locate the feeding of the five thousand in the context of Herod's murderous banquet. Mark specifically located the feeding of the 5,000 immediately after the birthday banquet thrown by Herod Antipas, the Roman king who was responsible for the region of Galilee. Herod's banquet was for politicians, high officials, military commanders and the leading men of Galilee.

The other was the people's banquet hosted by Jesus, and in attendance were the people of the soil, the wretched of the earth, the lumpen.

Mark was writing this Gospel from Rome and painted a picture of what life was like in the vast Roman Empire, where human beings had Babylonish oppressors with their knees on their necks and the people unable to breathe.

In Chapter 6, we are confronted with Roman taxation and its impact on the people of Galilee. Taxes derived from the Jews paid the cost for the maintenance of the presence of the occupying military force (those were the same military commanders at the banquet), and those taxes also paid for the elaborate banquet hosted by Herod. What selfishness! What a scandal! What a sin! What arrogance! What insensitivity! The oppressors were rubbing it in the face of hungry people.

We need a moral revolution to tackle issues of hunger, hardship and scandal. And what would a moral revolution look like? We must be aware of the enablers of evil, we must advocate on behalf of persons who are exploited and, finally, we must be active in the fight for equality.

BE AWARE OF THE ENABLERS OF EVIL

> *"The king was greatly distressed, but because of his oaths and his dinner guests, he did not want to refuse her."*
> *(Mark 6:26 NIV)*

To be aware of the enablers of evil, we need moral awareness, moral sensitivity and moral astuteness. This will help us to detect who the enablers and encouragers of evil are. Then, we will discern who are the people empowering evil, facilitating evil and promoting evil.

Paul said that our fight is not against flesh and blood, but against principalities and powers, against rulers and authority, against spiritual wickedness in high places (Eph. 6). Often, we focus on earthly evildoers and concentrate on the depraved personalities. However, there are forces behind politicians, private sector leaders, police, press people, preachers, public officials and public relations practitioners. What we see is not all there is to see. Here in this story in Mark, if we are not careful, we may concentrate on Salome the dancer, or on Herodias who hated John the Baptist for saying to Herod that it was not lawful for him to marry her, as she had been his brother's wife, or we may focus on Herod, a man with a family history of senseless violence against unarmed people. However, Herod was driven by his base, his loyal supporters and his hard-core "party people". They were the enablers. They held Herod captive. Herod was a puppet. The guests were the enablers of evil who had Herod on a string.

So, Mark does not ultimately lay the blame for the demise of John the Baptist at Salome's feet or Herodias' feet or even Herod's feet; he lays it at the feet of Herod's dinner guests: "The king was greatly distressed, but because of his oaths and his dinner guests, he did not want to refuse her" (Mark 6: 26 NIV). The dinner guests were the enablers. Herod had to please and impress his dinner guests. He had to keep his word to the dinner guests. Herod as a politician knew the value of "a promise made and a promise kept". The dinner guests were the enablers of corruption and crime. They were hungry for blood.

Be aware of the enablers on whom the system relies. Nothing happens without their approval. They do not say a word, nor do they need to; but their henchmen and "fixers" know what to do. They are the power elite. They are the promoters of corruption, although their hands are never caught in the cookie jar. They facilitate and organize crime, but their fingerprints are never on the illegal gun. They provoke chaos, but are never seen at the location of mayhem.

Be aware of these enablers who believe that they and their clique, their class and their colour have a divine right and manifest destiny to rule and to "lord it over" people who live in the "garrisons". For them, too much is never enough. Be aware and know how the system works and what makes the system work. Know their names, mark their faces and shame them.

And the greatest enabler of all is Satan. The enablers are the devil's advocates. That is why Jesus said to Peter, "Get thee behind me, Satan" (Matt. 16: 23 KJV). Peter was just echoing the devil's thoughts. Be aware of Satan, the power behind the evil throne. It is important that we understand who and what we are up against.

We must know them and identify them for who and what they are. Be aware of the enablers of evil, and the patron of evil, Satan.

ADVOCATE ON BEHALF OF PERSONS WHO ARE EXPLOITED

> *"[H]e had compassion on them because they were...*
> *like sheep without a shepherd." (Matt. 9:36 NIV)*

In Luke 4:16-18, Jesus declared his mission was to help the exploited people by proclaiming good news to the poor; proclaiming freedom to prisoners; recovering the sight of the blind; and setting the oppressed free. Because Jesus was advocating on behalf of persons who were exploited, what happened as a result was that the people in the synagogue were furious and they got up, drove him out of town in order to throw him off the cliff (Luke 4: 28-29). Be prepared to face criticism, even in the church, when we speak up on behalf of and side with the exploited people.

Bob Marley asked in "Redemption Song", "How long shall they kill our prophets / While we stand aside and look?" (1980). If we are going to speak up for persons who are exploited, then show moral courage. All four gospels have the phrase "be not afraid". This showed that moral courage was of paramount importance in being a Christian.

John the Baptist publicly frowned on the personal lifestyle of the powerful King Herod and Queen Herodias. That was moral courage. Elijah showed moral courage when he confronted King Ahab and his wife, Jezebel, who had confiscated Naboth's vineyard. Who will risk challenging the powers that be on behalf of the exploited? Baptist heroes Sam Sharpe, Paul Bogle and George William Gordon have left us a rich heritage of moral advocacy and courage. "Time come" for us to display again advocacy and courage on behalf of the voiceless, powerless people.

Some Christians will never say anything bad about you, whether before your face or behind your back. And that is good. However, those same Christians would never say anything in your defence when you are being exploited or falsely accused. That is cowardice and very bad. Always have the moral courage to advocate on behalf of persons who are exploited.

Advocate on behalf of those people, especially women, who are sexually harassed and who cannot get promoted because they refuse the sexual advances of their bosses. Advocate for women who refuse unwelcome sexual advances that made them feel intimidated and uncomfortable. Advocate that women be given more than one year to report a complaint of sexual harassment. The reality is that if a male politician sexually harasses a female and she reports it, she will be victimized, and chances are she will never get a legitimate job anywhere in Jamaica. Perhaps, she might have to wait until after that politician is out of office to report sexual harassment. We know the "runnings". We say advocate for victims, and especially our sexually harassed women who need more time to make a report.

In addition, we support the needy hungry people. Plead the cause of persons who are poor and needy (Prov. 31:9). Therefore, advocate on behalf of the customers who will be caught in a debt trap for taking food on hire purchase. Let us emulate the age-old practice of community shops which offered credit or "trust" for food items which would allow the customer to settle the debt on payday without interest. Advocate for the exploited to get interest-free food packages.

Friends, let us follow our moral compass and be resolute in our moral advocacy, in the name of God on behalf of our exploited sisters and brothers, and then when all is said, we take moral action.

BE ACTIVE IN THE FIGHT FOR EQUALITY

"You give them something to eat." (Mark 6:37 NIV)

What does the moral revolution consist of, in light of the evil structural, institutional, fiscal and monetary mechanism that is legislated by the ruling class? What does a moral revolution do in the face of the abuse of power? A moral revolution leads to activism in the fight for equal treatment for all.

Awareness is good and advocacy is better, but the best is when the church implements specific actions on behalf of the people, based on the value of equality of all. Jesus heard about the public, callous beheading of John, and about the open display of opulence at the banquet, and he was moved with compassion for a hopeless, helpless and hapless crowd, and gave them a word, hope, food and a future.

The need is great and urgent, and so we have to take action. With the help of God, it is time for us to use the little bit of fish and bread to accomplish much. Rise up and give people hope, bread, fish and a future. The moral revolution requires us to treat all people with dignity and civility. Serve people compassionately and personally. We do not scorn anyone. We do not stigmatize anyone. We support people who are weak. If there is one place where we "guard each person's dignity and save each person's pride" (Words from the song *They'll Know We Are Christians By Our Love*), it must be in the community of faith, the church. Every human being should be regarded with respect and caressed with care in the household of faith. Everybody else may see colour, creed, class, disease or status. But in here, we observe equality, and we outdo one another in showing honour. We must first see their humanity and their need. Let us help especially those who are neglected by the State.

Fellow activists, in the name of God, in the name of what is right and in the name of our brothers and sisters in need of food, help someone as we travel along. Then, our living shall not be in vain. It is a disgrace when food spoils in our fridges, or the expiry date has passed on edibles in our pantries, and then we throw away the food. What a waste. We should share our food with the less fortunate, and "give them something to eat". Support Boulevard Baptist's Care Basket and the 100 people we feed monthly. Support the Boulevard Baptist's soup kitchen. COVID-19 makes people's living conditions worse, so it is not time to cut back, but to feed more needy people while protecting their dignity. It is time for action based on equality.

- Start a moral revolution by being aware of the enablers of evil.
- Start a moral revolution by advocating on behalf of the exploited.
- Start a moral revolution by being active based on equality of all.

Conclusion

And then there is coming the Messianic banquet where Jesus the host will say to us:

> Come and see the table spread for you.
> Come, those who have no money and buy wine.
> Come, those who labour and are heavy laden,
> and rest at this banquet.
> Come, those who received bad things in this earthly life,
> and enjoy milk and honey,
> Come and let me anoint your head with oil
> and make your cup overflow.
> Come, those who used to beg for crumbs from rich men's tables,

and enjoy daily bread from the Lord's table.
At this banquet, there will be music and dancing;
there will be no more tears or sorrows.
Come and eat the fatted calf,
and dress up in robes and wear a ring.
Come, those have gone through great tribulation.

Come to this all-day party,
because there will be no more night.
Come and see your loved ones
somewhere around the banquet table.

Because we have that hope, we fear no one in this life; we know the enablers of evil, and we are going to advocate on behalf of the exploited and take action based on the value of equality of all, and we will feed all hungry people.

PRAY TO THE LORD

Scripture Lesson: Matthew 6:1-13
"Our Father who art in Heaven…" (Matt. 6:9 ASV)

» 5 July 2020

Recently, a cabinet minister, in a video clip, said of the government, "we are overwhelmed with COVID-19 and crime", and he asked for prayers. Many of us can identify with this cabinet minister's feeling of being overwhelmed. We feel overwhelmed by many obstacles, over-stressed because of complications, and we sometimes feel "out of it" because of missed opportunities, and underwhelmed by our dismal performance. Therefore, let us turn our eyes to the Lord's Prayer: to learn again how to pray, to learn what is prayer and what to pray about, and perchance it might deepen and enhance our lives, and help us to handle the pressures of life and problems in life.

When the disciples of Jesus saw that their prayer lives were lacking, although they knew about praying, they humbled themselves and asked Jesus to teach them to pray. They saw also the difference in the prayer life of Jesus and the oneness between the Father and the Son, and they wanted that quality relationship through praying. They wanted something more out of prayer and wanted something different from life. So, Jesus taught them how to pray and how not to pray, and Jesus taught them what to pray for and what not to pray for.

Jesus said, do not pray as a performance with many words and many vain repetitions, nor in places where one can be seen. He also said do not pray like non-believers who pray asking for things, as if God does not know what is needed before we pray.

Instead, pray realizing that God, "Our Father", is our family, is friendly, and delights in pouring out his favour on all his children. The entire Lord's Prayer hinges on "Our Father" and the rest of the Lord's Prayer is an explanation, expansion and exposition of the idea "Our Father". What are the implications of God being "Our Father"? Because he is "Our Father" he will provide for us daily food; because he is "Our Father" he forgives us our trespasses; because he is "Our Father" he protects us from the Evil One. Because he is "Our Father" he empowers us to minister so that his will be done on earth, as it is in heaven. Because he is "Our Father" we can communicate with him and commune with him in a very close and intimate relationship – he is not a stranger; he is not far removed; he is not missing in action. Because he is "Our Father", then we are all one family. We are all sisters and brothers. Being able to call God, the all-powerful, all-knowing God, "Our Father" is the most awesome thing in the world and the best relationship we can have.

This Lord's Prayer is significant because Jesus created this prayer and taught this prayer. The Lord's Prayer was very important because the one who prays best, and knew all the secrets about praying, designed it. This prayer came from the lips of Jesus and reflected the lifestyle of Jesus.

The Lord's Prayer is special because it created a bond between God and Jesus' disciples, similar to the bond between Jesus and his Father.

This prayer, which is significant and special, should be a priority in our Christian life. This prayer is useful and valuable for private meditation, personal use and public consumption. Therefore, preserve the integrity of the Lord's Prayer. Put your trust in God, "Our Father", for protection from the Evil One, and pass on the Lord's Prayer to a needy and worried world.

Pray to the Lord

Preserve the Integrity of the Lord's Prayer

Since the Lord's Prayer is significant and special, then we must preserve the integrity of the Lord's Prayer from misuse and misunderstanding.

We must preserve the integrity and the wholesomeness of the Lord's Prayer from those who want to make it a public performance. Praying to "Our Father" is not about improving our image or status. It is not about who is seeing us on live streaming when we pray. Praying is not a time to exhibit ourselves.

Preserve the integrity, soundness and truthfulness of the Lord's Prayer from those who feel that praying is about petitioning God about our earthly needs only. It is not primarily for informing God about what we need. God knows our every need before we pray: "Your Father knoweth what things ye have need of, before ye ask him" (Matt. 6:8 KJV). God knows our needs more than we know our needs. In other words, even if someone does not pray for daily food, God still provides out of his goodness and graciousness. Praying to God is not praying to someone who is ignorant about our needs.

We must preserve the integrity of the Lord's Prayer against those who put the creature before the Creator. The Lord's Prayer is saying that it is Jesus who is Lord, and not Herod or Pilate or the emperor with all their power, possessions, pomp and pride. Saying that the prayer emanates from the Lord Jesus is a political statement. It goes against the grain of political order that seeks unquestioned loyalty and obedience to politicians, policemen, preachers, parents, private sector leaders and public figures. Every time we pray the Lord's Prayer, we are making a political statement that God is in charge, and not US president Donald Trump or Russian president Vladimir Putin. The Lord's Prayer is a political prayer, because it goes against the greed of the world and reminds us to trust God for daily supplies. The Lord's Prayer reminds us that it is our Father who ultimately supplies our needs, and not our employers who pay us; it is ultimately God who protects us, and not the police and soldiers.

Additionally, preserving the integrity of the Lord's Prayer is ensuring that everyone understands that the essence of praying is communicating and communing with God. The goal and purpose of praying is about communication and communion with "Our Father". Communicating with God is more than talking to God with words. Someone who cannot speak can communicate with God. Communicating with God is about being in communion with God, whether through words, nonverbal signs, sighs and tears. It is a sharing of our minds and emotions with God – our souls touching the being of God and the being of God touching our souls. The essence, purpose and goal of prayer is communion. Jesus said, "I am in the Father and the Father is in me" (John 14:11 NIV). This is why the Pharisees wanted to kill Jesus: because of the intimacy Jesus had with the Father through prayer. And Jesus wanted the disciples to have that same oneness experience: "Abide in me, and I in you" (John 15:4 KJV). When we commune with God as friend with friend then we:

Discern the will of God for our lives, and then our will becomes God's will, so that God's will may be done on earth as it is in heaven. Prayer allows us to experience a little heaven on earth.

- We depend on God, and then God can depend on us.
- We desire God, and our desires become God's desires.
- We hunger and thirst after righteousness, and God reveals his counsel to us.

When we commune with God in prayer, it is possible to experience closeness with God. Praying has its ultimate goal, that Christ dwells in us and we dwell in Jesus. This wonder-working relationship will make us known to God, and God will be confident to share with us his secrets.

Preserving the integrity of the Lord's Prayer is about communicating with "Our Father", communion with the Spirit, and closeness with Jesus.

PUT YOUR FAITH IN 'OUR FATHER' GOD FOR PROTECTION

As we communicate with God and commune with God, as friend with friend, then we will realize that God does not want us to be trapped and tricked in the places and spaces of temptation. We can test for evil in our lives, we can trace evil in our lives, we can get treated for evil, and we can get rid of evil from our lives.

We will also be able to say, "Though I walk through the valley of the shadow of death, I will fear no evil" (Ps. 23:4). Rely on God for protection, and he will deliver us from the Evil One, the evil system, evil spirits and the evildoers.

Pray to the Lord

The devil uses diseases to frighten us, cramp us and paralyze us. Dade County in Florida has a population of 2.7 million, almost as large as the population of Jamaica, but while we had 10 deaths that are COVID-19 related, they have had 10,000 deaths, but we are more scared than the people in Florida. Why are some members not in church? Is it out of fear and lack of faith? Some people go to the supermarket, the hairdresser, to nine nights for politicians, and to Western Union more than they are willing to go to church. Careful that the Evil One is not using diseases to scare us.

The Evil One is the author and finisher of discrimination. Put your faith in God so that the devil will not lead us to engage in discrimination. Once we genuinely pray and say "Our Father", then we cannot discriminate along the lines of race, sex, age, class and creed. Our Father means we are all related to one Father. Anybody who is part of a divisive clique in this church or any other church does not know and understand the "Our Father" of the Lord's Prayer.

There is a school of thought, which I subscribe to, which says that if there is a very great worker, but the person is not keeping the unity of the Spirit and the church, and is divisive, then get rid of the worker. However, if Christians are not great workers, not talented workers, but they are keeping God's unity, then keep them and work with them. Keep the ones who are unifiers who preserve the unity of the Spirit. Understand that this prayer is about unity of the Body of Christ under "Our Father".

Put your trust in "Our Father", knowing He protects the unity of the Church.

Pass on the Lord's Prayer

Through the Lord's Prayer, we are able to experience oneness with God and commune with him as friend with friend. We should then be able to tell others about the Lord's Prayer, and teach the Lord's Prayer to others. What are we going to share about the Lord's Prayer? It is this. God knows our every need before we ask. What are we going to share about the Lord's Prayer? It is also this. Praying the Lord's Prayer is about communicating with God and communion with God as friend with friend. Pass on the idea that praying to "Our Father" facilitates a close relationship with God.

What else are we going to share about the Lord's Prayer? Revd Dr Horace Russell, retired Baptist minister and brother to foundation member Sister Dorleen Williams, in preaching on the Lord's Prayer after the 9/11 attacks in New York and Washington DC, said that the Lord's Prayer was used as a secret code in which the early Christians recognized each other during turbulent, dangerous and evil persecution. So, let us share with others that the Lord's Prayer is a source of comfort; a source of hope; a source of strength in times of trouble, trials and tribulations. Tell others that through praying we are more than conquerors. Let us pass it on.

Conclusion

God gives us the privilege to pray to him and He also expects that we accept the responsibility to preserve the Lord's Prayer and pass it on. Pass on the valuable and useful Lord's Prayer to a needy world.

Figure 2. "No Mask, No Service" Sign at the Entrance of an Episcopal Church

Photograph by Devon Dick (7 June 2020)

Figure 3. Devon Dick Preaching at 2018 JBU Assembly
Photograph by Dennis Duncan (21 February 2018)

TWO
PRESIDENTIAL PROCLAMATIONS

LIVING IN PARTNERSHIP
JAMAICA BAPTIST UNION ASSEMBLY
OPENING SERVICE 2018

Scripture Lesson: Romans 12:1-21

» *21 February 2018*

This opening service will be the first public event to launch our two-year theme, "Living in Partnership". Our text Romans 12:3-5 states: 'For by the grace given me I say to every one of you: Do not think of yourself more highly than you ought, but rather think of yourself with sober judgment, in accordance with the faith God has distributed to each of you. For just as each of us has one body with many members, and these members do not all have the same function, so in Christ we, though many, form one body, and each member belongs to all the others" (NIV).

In 1783, some 235 years ago, George Liele, an American Black man, and his wife Hannah established Baptist work and witness in Jamaica with a commitment to living in partnership with all. Liele was committed to partnership between women and men, demonstrated through his having an equal number of male and female elders (12 women and 12 men) to partner with him for the pastoral oversight of the congregation. In addition, his congregation consisted of Blacks and Whites. He was committed to racial harmony. Furthermore, he

Two • Presidential Proclamations

invited missionaries from the Baptist Union of Great Britain to help with the growing pastoral work, at the same time as he embraced the Anabaptist tradition, a tradition, which the Baptist Union of Great Britain detested. He drew from diverse traditions to the glory of God. We could say Liele was the first successful pastor among the enslaved because he affirmed partnership, and his life and ministry were characterized by living in partnership.

This passage from Romans 12 shows the link between the sub-theme we embraced for the past two years, "Living the Sacrificial Life": "I beseech you therefore, brethren, by the mercies of God, that ye present your bodies a living sacrifice" (Rom. 12:1 KJV), and also the sub-theme for these next two years, "Living in Partnership" (Rom. 12:3-5). A life of ongoing self-giving commitment in shared relationship with the body is the solid basis and enduring foundation for meaningful and effective partnership. This becomes possible when, as far as the Christian is concerned, both the life transforming mercies of God and the pattern of Christ's own saving sacrificial giving of himself are accepted by grace through faith in Jesus. This is exactly what the apostle is laying out to the community of faith in this most important passage of scripture. Paul sees this as an urgent necessity and possibility warranted by the very nature and character of the calling of God's people in the world. It is the opportunity of grace granted for the people of God to make a contribution that only they can make.

We are therefore reminded in our text that such a necessity and possibility is not going to be accomplished through the efforts of isolated individualism, self-sufficient partisan group efforts or divisive power struggles after the manner of the world. There was early warning against conformity to the world (Rom. 12:2) with its misplaced values and priorities, which produce the levels of disruptive, destructive and self-defeating strategies that we have become accustomed to, and have been presented with as answers to our perennial human problems.

Paul desired Jews and Gentiles to peacefully coexist in the same church because Jesus has brought into being by his death and resurrection a new community. We should therefore build partnerships based on at least four pillars:

- Partnership requires humility
- Partnership requires valuing dignity

Living in Partnership

- Partnership requires maintaining civility
- Partnership requires embracing community

If I may say so, these are the values, which, to one degree or another, we are called to establish, demonstrate and affirm – everyone in our midst – with the church giving a moral lead. I ask with deep sincerity, how do we see ourselves in the light of humility, dignity, civility and in light of the community to which I now speak?

We are urged to engage in the practice of **HUMILITY**. As Paul puts it, "Do not think of yourself more highly than you ought, but rather think of yourself with sober judgment" (Rom. 12:3 NIV).

Partnership requires humility. The first pillar of partnership is practising humility. In order to practise humility, we need to get rid of exaggerated notions of ourselves, our class, our church, our group, our political party, our school ties, and so on.

Arrogance, egotism, dogmatism in relation to the influence we believe we wield, our reliance on the knowledge or expertise we have garnered, the power, gifts or talents we perceive ourselves to have, the positions we hold, or the people whom we know, or those who know us, are signs of lack of humility. Lack of humility breeds disrespect. Do we not need to hear this at every level in our society, and are we not aware of the impulses in our hearts, in our own circles? Can we separate certain of the disruptive factors we experience in our midst from the sheer arrogance, the sense of self-importance associated with common practice in certain key areas of our national and community life?

Here are some telltale signs that tend to reveal what we are warned against:

(a) The unwillingness to admit we are wrong, or the desire to claim we have been misunderstood when we are wrong. Beware!

(b) The unwillingness to listen to others who tell the truth we need to hear, not the deception we would prefer. Beware!

(c) The unwillingness to learn, especially from those with whom we are in disagreement, though we need to. Beware!

Putting it positively, what humility does mean and involve is a willingness to admit we are wrong when we are; a willingness to listen to others who will and can tell us what we need to do, and not

TWO ● Presidential Proclamations

necessarily just what we want to hear; a willingness to learn from others, even those with whom we disagree or who disagree with us.

Do not be mistaken. Humility does not mean demeaning ourselves or being lacking in confidence in self, nor feeling that all things foreign are inherently better than the local. It is not about self-denigration. It is not belittling ourselves or feeling inferior to others who have more possessions and have achieved more in life.

Lieutenant Stitchie, before he became a gospel artiste, had a song "Wear Yu Size" (1987) in which he relates a story about a woman with size 10 feet who tried to wear size 8. Let us overlook the anti-woman message of the song and get the message of the importance of sober judgment in assessing our own real size. Humility calls for wearing "yu size", the right size, making the right assessment, not too high and not too low.

Humility is a sober assessment of one's abilities and achievements; one's own limitations and vulnerabilities; and one's constant need of God's grace in order to be humble. Furthermore, when we are truly humble, one's own personal story is never a priority in the service of the common good. This is a call for humility, which is truly not heard often enough, but for partnership to work it requires being built upon a pillar of humility.

Partnership Requires Valuing Dignity

The second pillar of partnership is valuing dignity. We must value our dignity and the dignity of others because we are all created in the image of God. What is dignity? Dignity is the state or quality of being worthy of honour and respect. The sober judgment that is therefore associated with humility will lead to valuing dignity. This will be judgement based not on mere posture, poise or pose. Dignity is not based simply on office held, the trappings provided by possessions, or the effects of good public relations team. Dignity does not have a human origin. It is of God. Dignity is a gift from God to each one of us. No one has more dignity than another person. It is a sacred divine endowment granted by our having been created in the image of God. Therein lies the sanctity of human dignity upon which rests the immeasurable worth of every single human being, barring none. All humans are equal in dignity. The implications of this are vast.

Attacks upon inherent human dignity comprise one of the greatest acts of human presumptuousness that could be displayed. It is a choice to devalue that upon which God has conferred the highest value possible. It is a way of playing God, taking over from God, and flying in the face of God. This is the basis of cruelties, insensitivity, senseless slaughter, self-centred sex, wickedness, corruption, exploitation and indifference against fellow human beings. It is an attempt to disregard, deface and mar the ones who were created to reflect most accurately who God is.

(1) It is a sin to deprive a human being of the basic necessities conducive to living a life of viable dignity.

(2) It is wicked to label, stereotype, classify and categorize people in order to demean God's creations.

(3) It is wrong to call Nikolas Cruz who killed 17 former school mates in Florida a monster. We might say he behaved like a monster, but never call someone made in the image of God a monster. Cruz has dignity because he was made in the image of God. We value his inherent dignity in spite of what he has done. Paradoxically, we would not call Paul, the writer of Romans, a monster, but he engaged in some awful acts and the blood of saints were on his hands when he was Saul the persecutor. So, as we respect the dignity of Paul, respect Cruz's also.

Therefore, if we are setting basic standards for people in prison or detention, we must be guided by what is in line with the dignity of being human.

Remember each human being is a creature with dignity no matter what he or she has done or failed to do, or what was done to him or her. Human dignity is not measured based on achievement, attainment or any human assessment.

We of the majority Black population of this nation know that it was the sense of their human dignity that our enslaved and oppressed ancestors were not willing to relinquish, and that formed the basis and source of the resistance that was integral to their liberation. This is an enduring legacy. Where are our acts of advocacy? What are we doing today? Where is our voice? Where are the projects that serve as evidence of our continued commitment to defending, promoting and advancing the value of human dignity? Are we comfortable with citing evidence of the past centuries of what we have done as a church to justify our present level of effectiveness? We need the appropriate humanizing health, education, and welfare enabling projects and programmes to give meaning to this.

TWO ● PRESIDENTIAL PROCLAMATIONS

To live in wholesome partnership, we require valuing our dignity and the dignity of all others.

PARTNERSHIP REQUIRES MAINTAINING CIVILITY

The first pillar of partnership is humility. The second pillar of partnership is valuing dignity, and the third pillar of partnership requires us maintaining civility. Dignity is a gift from God to us, civility is a gift from each person to the other in the way we treat each other. Being civil is showing or giving respect and honour to each other.

Civility is the respect, the honour, due and accorded by a human being to a fellow human being as just that – a fellow human, first and foremost and above all of God's creation. This is separate and apart from acknowledged achievements and attainments in this world, and amongst peers. This is also in spite of and despite ways in which they might have proven themselves failures or caused great disappointment due to the manner in which they have chosen to live their lives. Maintaining civility is the sign of a truly responsible, maturing and mature society that the church must participate in building.

Incivility, such as rudeness and crudeness, and coarseness and hooliganism, is inconsistent with the practice of humility and the valuing of human dignity. A critical indicator of the level of social disorder is the degree of incivility manifested in the society. Public discourse, social media communication, religious debate, conduct at church and in assembly meetings, our sharing of public facilities, and our use of the roads are often done with incivility. Incivility manifests itself also in ignoring a fellow human, teasing someone and vilifying a sister or brother. The temptation is to disrupt the partnership by showing a lack of respect, particularly if we feel that we are better than others and more important than others. Maintaining civility is not a matter of convenience or preference, and is not calculated in terms of self-interest, because civility is something due to everyone without exception. Authentic civility makes a statement about the kind of human beings we are.

Can the current senseless slaughter of humans divorced from the incivility with which we treat others? We say incivility is connected to gang violence, political violence, community violence and drug violence. In 1996, Horace Levy, public policy professional, along with other researchers went into five volatile urban areas to study poverty-related violence and discovered that the residents wanted outsiders to respect them and not to stigmatize them. (1996, 38). Unfortunately, the main resources of those five communities were drugs and guns when what they required was employment, sewage disposal, decent housing, community participation, an adequate support system and decision-making apparatus upon which community self-respect and morale can hinge. They wanted respect and they deserved it.

Respect can be afforded to all and offered by all. In the words of our national anthem: "Teach us true respect for all". Let us outdo one another in showing civility to all. Be courteous, be polite in remarks and actions, disagree without being disagreeable and disrespectful, if at all possible, seek win/win situations, and let our natural response be to seek common ground based on common humanity and, yes, maintain civility.

We are building partnership and there are four pillars of partnership. The first pillar of partnership requires humility, the second pillar of partnership requires dignity, the third pillar of partnership requires civility, and now the fourth pillar of partnership requires embracing community. Finally, live in partnership through **EMBRACING COMMUNITY** "so in Christ we, though many, form one body, and each member belongs to all the others" (Rom. 12:5 NIV).

The danger of "divide and rule" has been a part of our historical legacy that we must now abandon. Our willingness to give up the "divide and rule" approach will be a critical sign of our liberty and maturity. Our "crab in a barrel mentality" of engaging in a "fight for scarce benefits and spoils carried on by hostile tribes that seem to be perpetually at war" (P.J. Patterson, former PM) affects community living. Our scorched earth attitude of "if I can't have it, neither can you" destroys community. We cannot live in partnership based on divide and rule practices, the crab in a barrel mentality or scorched earth attitudes. We often spend a lot of time denying our need for community and for each other, which results in much of our relational disunity, disorder, and dysfunctionality.

Embracing community is to affirm our interrelatedness. Interrelatedness is about the relationship among the past, the present and the future. Past actions affect the present and have future consequences. So, when we have spent future earnings, which affects generations unborn, or consume while expecting future generations to pay, then we fail to grasp or are insensitive to how our actions affect those coming behind us. Embracing community means being sensitive to

TWO ○ PRESIDENTIAL PROCLAMATIONS

the aspirations of future generations and planning long-term. Embracing community is about our interrelatedness.

Embracing community is also about our interdependence. Living in partnership implies that we need each other, we are reliant on each other and we ought to enrich each other. It is only when each person contributes by availing himself and his talents that the body of Christ's church functions optimally. In community we are therefore not primarily competitors, but we complement each other so that we may achieve completeness, fullness and inclusiveness. Interdependence means we recognize that labour needs capital and capital needs labour; the Jamaica Labour Party (JLP) needs the People's National Party (PNP) and the PNP needs the JLP; companies need customers and customers need companies; Jamaica needs the rest of the Caribbean and the Caribbean needs Jamaica; Kingston College (KC) needs Calabar and Calabar needs KC. The value of community living is seen in that famous quote "All for one and one for all" from Alexandre Dumas' novel *The Three Musketeers*. As the Jamaican proverb says, "one han' cyaan clap". You cannot do it alone. You have to work with others to achieve a common goal.

What is the foundation on which to build a community? For a community to be strong, sustainable and effective, it must be a community of equals. There has to be equality in status, dignity, rights and access to resources and opportunities on a fair basis. But is Jamaica committed to equality or promoting equality, and are we willing to create policies driven by equality?

According to the president of the Private Sector Organisation of Jamaica (PSOJ), Howard Mitchell, equality is not in the philosophy and practice of political parties. And after being a member of every major political party (JLP, PNP and the National Democratic Movement, or NDM) he concluded that "the plantation system is still with us... the political parties have perpetuated a system of hierarchy that replicates the plantation. The political parties have not engendered equality... for the most part encouraging division" (Serju 6 Dec. 2017). We have not heard anyone challenging Mitchell's analysis of the political parties. So, it is spot on. He should, however, give some credit where credit is due and state who created the plantation mentality of inequality, and give paternity to the forebears of the PSOJ. In addition, many sections of the 19th century church sanctified this plantation culture of inequality.

Inequality anywhere is a threat to equality in community everywhere. Deep down, we crave exemptions, waivers, fringe benefits and spoils not based on merit, but solely because of our connections. We need people who are open to change as we strive for equality in community.

Paul in 1 Corinthians 3 was at pains to emphasize that the workers, whether those who plant or water, are coequals. Again, Paul returns to the theme of equality by using the imagery of the body to show that the various parts – mouth, anus, hands and eyes – are of equal value, worth and dignity. We are equal before God in the value of our ministry.

What is another fundamental value on which to build community? We need to accept our diversity. 1 Cor. 3 reminds us of the plurality of members and diversity of gifts. Since God made us, accepts us and appreciates us all with our differences in personality, colour and orientation, then in the name of community development, we ought to accept one another, without first requesting and requiring everyone else to become like us or feeling a need for us to become like others. Embracing community is accepting togetherness in plurality, not just living side by side; it is appreciating each other's diversity, not tolerating only. Embracing community is all about the shared life of belongingness.

Embracing community means affirming our equality and accepting our diversity. When we embrace community, then certain events or actions follow as day follows night. And what is that? There will be a passion for ecumenism and a pursuit of church unity consistent with the prayer of Jesus in John 17. Embracing community is one of the critical areas in which the collective church could and should give a clear spiritual and moral lead. Is the present state of church unity a reflection of this? Do we believe in the effective power of a profound moral example? Can we say that our circuit, our denomination, our ecumenical movement create a pattern of community which we can call the nation and society to emulate? Let us reaffirm and embrace ecumenism.

What happens when we affirm community? It is this. There will be a passion for evangelism and a pursuit of evangelism. All human beings within the community, irrespective of colour, class or creed, need Jesus.

What else happens when we are committed to community? We have a passion for and we pursue egalitarianism in our relationships

TWO ● Presidential Proclamations

and the provision of opportunities for persons who are disabled, need long-term care, are disadvantaged and discriminated against, and the diseased.

The outworking of embracing community living will be a lifetime of commitment to ecumenism, evangelism and an egalitarian society. It is to affirm a community of equals and to respect our diversity. It is to embrace our interdependence and interrelatedness.

Conclusion

What are we saying? It is critical that we have the basic pillars to build a wholesome partnership that can realize the objectives of Vision 2030 of Jamaica becoming the place of choice to live, work, raise families and do business. We are offering four pillars of partnership, which are seen in these declarations: partnership requires humility, partnership requires valuing dignity, partnership requires maintaining civility and partnership requires embracing community. These values and virtues do not get better over time or by chance, but by intentionality and purposeful actions. We ought to deliberately affirm living in partnership through humility, dignity, civility and community.

Perhaps the greatest example of partnership ever in the history of Jamaica occurred in December 1831, when a humble man, one who valued the dignity of the enslaved and who embraced community based on equality of all and solidarity with all, one who maintained civility of respect, a pastor of his congregation with no civil or legal or political rights, Sam Sharpe, mobilized approximately 60,000 enslaved or one-fifth of the total population of the island in a passive resistance against conditions of slavery, and ultimately made a significant difference in Jamaica and the Caribbean in the areas of politics, church and social relations. Sharpe built on the foundation laid by Hannah and George Liele and has left us a rich legacy. As we take the baton, being God's people in God's world and continue on the path to "living in partnership" – partnership with God and our fellow human beings – our paradigm stands on the pillars of practising humility, valuing dignity, maintaining civility and embracing community.

WITNESSING FERVENTLY
2018 JAMAICA BAPTIST UNION ASSEMBLY

> **Scripture Lesson: John 4: 27-42**
> *"Lift up your eyes, and look on the fields; for they are white already to harvest"* (John 4:35 KJV).

» *26 February 2017*

Earlier this month, I visited an establishment and sought and received a favour from a worker. In return, I invited him to attend church. In addition, because I knew the owner of the company is a Baptist, I encouraged him to talk to the owner about his spiritual life and journey. He said that this Baptist Christian worker was not interested in his spiritual life. The owner had never invited him to church. All the owner wanted to know was that the work was done and done properly. Some Christians do not recognize that witnessing ought to be part and parcel of their daily activities and lives.

We have no reason to exist apart from being a Jesus people, a Jesus movement and a Jesus community, engaged in witnessing fervently. One of the definitive and distinctive features of our life and existence in this regard, is that we are entrusted participants in the mission of Jesus Himself. In the Gospel of John, Jesus underscores this. He unreservedly and trustingly indicated to his disciples that they were stewards of the same mission: "As you sent me into the world, I have sent them into the world" (John 17:18 NIV). Jesus had confidence in his disciples. Again, Jesus in a post-resurrection scene reminded the overjoyed disciples about his and their mission: "Jesus said, 'Peace be with you! As the Father has sent me, I am sending you'" (John 20:21 NIV). In faithfulness to this missional task, we as the Jamaica Baptist Union, part of the Jesus people, part of the Jesus movement, and part of the Jesus community, have set ourselves to pursue the missional task as our life's purpose.

We believe that the story of the encounter between Jesus and the Samaritan woman is as good and valuable as any, and more pointed and compelling than many, in offering insights into the pattern of mission that Jesus has entrusted to us. We stand in great disobedience and unfaithfulness if we would not heed its call and challenge.

TWO ● PRESIDENTIAL PROCLAMATIONS

This Samaritan woman undertook the challenge to engage in the mission of Jesus and witnessed to the townsfolk and planted a church in Samaria.

Jesus wanted his disciples to have that sort of "Woman at the Well" passion and attitude, hence he said to them, "Lift up your eyes, and look on the fields; for they are white already to harvest" (John 4:35 KJV). Jesus used the symbolism of the harvest of corn fields to call and challenge the disciples to undertake this urgent mission, because the people were ripe for believing in God. Jesus challenged the disciples to lift up their eyes from their food and their bellies, to look outward, and to stay on the mission of witnessing fervently.

The call is to witness fervently. To witness is to testify about what has been revealed to us in community by God's Spirit, God's Son, God's scriptures and God's saints, and also a willingness to suffer and die in the ministry of the Gospel of Jesus. The word "martyr" is a transliteration of the Greek word for witness, implying that a true witness must be willing to die for the cause. This must be done passionately and with intensity. Our goal for Mission 2020 drives us to "lift up [your] eyes, look on the fields; for they are white already to harvest" (John 4:35 KJV). Therefore, we go OUT as reapers to reap not our harvest but God's harvest. Today, we encourage you to accept the call, command, commission and challenge to undertake what we want to call PROJECT OUT, with O.U.T. being an acronym: O for Outward; and U for Urgent and T for Thrust – an Outward Urgent Thrust.

OUTWARD (A PREOCCUPATION WITH OTHERS)

The disciples of Jesus seemed to make a reasonable and legitimate point to Jesus concerning his need for food. The great temptation for Jesus was the seeming reasonableness of the position. It was similar in nature to the reasonableness of the devil's suggestion to Jesus who was hungry after being in the wilderness for forty days and forty nights. Again, Jesus was called upon to be distracted by self-serving preoccupation. No one could argue with a hungry man seeking by whatever means necessary to satisfy that hunger. Not so with Jesus, because he was not inward looking. For Jesus, it was not firstly and primarily about his needs, comforts and safety. Jesus saw the inward focus of the disciples as standing in the way of opportunities that were on the horizon for missional activity.

Truth be told, when a choice has to be made, we are faced with a similar dilemma thinking about and being preoccupied with seemingly reasonable and legitimate comforts, compensation, salary and safety over and against a missional task which beckons us, and might be a once-in-a-lifetime opportunity. Is it not true that sometimes we get preoccupied with inward-looking matters at the expense of an outward vision? Do we not sometimes become parochial rather than looking outward? Yes, we get distracted with self-serving, self-absorbed preoccupations with such things as internal programmes and concerns, like spending more on fixtures, buildings, conveniences, internal meetings rather than outreach programmes, rather than responding to genuine "outward" needs. We try to justify our position of "inwardness" only by philosophizing that we have to learn to "dance a yard" first before we go abroad. Check how much of our yearly budgeted expenditure has been spent on ourselves? Reread our minutes from council, members' and deacons' meetings and see how much of our discussions relate to in-house issues. What if we did a survey on the various ministries in our congregations, would we discover that inward-looking services were strong and evangelism was weak? We are becoming a "selfie" church; we are saying "look at me now". We are blinded by our own beauty.

Unfortunately, even sometimes when we have the outward look it is an outward look that is admiration only, envy mainly and selfish mostly? What are we talking about? Some look outwards in admiration only at what other denominations are doing well, and asking why the Jamaica Baptist Union cannot be like them without doing any self-critical analysis, and asking why we in our local setting and with our situation cannot emulate these good qualities and best practices. So, our outward-looking tendency of admiring others does not translate to desiring it for our context and what role we should play to make mission possible. Then there are those who look outward with envy at the good witnessing taking place over there. There is an underlying resentment and bitterness towards those who are faithful, and we explain their faithfulness as being due to their having greater human resources, greater financial resources and the infrastructure, space and contacts to do well, and we complain that we do not have those things, and hence we are not doing as well as them. So, we fail to see the potential and possibilities there are in our context with our resources and our spiritual gifts. One group looks outward with admiration for the wrong reasons and the other looks out with envy.

TWO ● PRESIDENTIAL PROCLAMATIONS

Perhaps, the worst tendency we have is engaging in networking for selfish inward-focused projects and ministry. We seek opportunities to influence and acquire friends in order that they will fund our internal and inward projects in the churches. We need an **outward vision**. We will see what can be, ought to be and what is possible and practical, what is reasonable and reachable. We also need to know what is this mission of the outward vision? The first thing we have to determine is: who is our target audience?

Unfortunately, we have created Jesus in our own image and fail to perceive the felt need as a basis for mission. The judgment scene in Matthew 25 catches the condemned people flat footed. Hence, they asked Jesus, "Lord, when did we see you hungry or thirsty or a stranger or needing clothes or sick or in prison, and did not help you?" (Matt. 25:44 NIV). The answer is that "whatever you did not do for one of the least of these, you did not do for me" (Matt. 25:45 NIV). They did not recognize the Christ in a human being who had a need. Persons in need were invisible people. We also pass them every day without seeing Jesus in them, and without feeling the need to present Jesus to them and to be Jesus to them. These are people who are hungry, thirsty, strangers, naked, sick and imprisoned. They ought to be the core, focus and heart of the mission.

According to William Temple (1881-1944), former Archbishop of Canterbury (1942-1944), "The Church is the only organization that does not exist for itself, but for those who live outside of it" (*New World Encyclopedia*). With that understanding of the mission, it is not surprising that Temple was instrumental in preparing the groundwork for the National Health Service and welfare support in the United Kingdom. If we had that same mission for outward ministry, we would accomplish more, and our ministry in the name of God would be different.

The mission is to outsiders, outcasts, outliers and outlandish people. Who are the outsiders? Those persons who are excluded, those who live on the periphery and in the margins. Then, who are the outcasts? Those who are disliked and discriminated against. Then, who are the outliers and outlandish people? These are they who are strangers and strange, who do not look like us, who do not dress like us, who do not eat like us, who do not walk like us, who do not talk like us and do not worship like us. In summary, they would be like intersex people whose reproductive anatomy does not seem to fit within the typical definition of male and female. This outward stretch will lead us to others: outsiders, outcasts, outliers and the outlandish people. Our database must not comprise of members only, but have a whole heap of outsiders, outcasts and outliers and outlandish people in it.

Since we have the vision of what ought to be, and since we know the mission is for others, then let us seize the moment. We need to go to these persons and present the gospel at an opportune time, such as in times of crisis or illness or reversals of fortune, confusion about decision making, and times of celebration like marriage, promotions and the birth of a child.

When we see Minister Marion Hall, aka "Lady Saw", and the "Queen of Dancehall", singing gospel songs and Mr Vegas, whose birth name is Clifford Smith, converting to Christianity soon after releasing his 2016 dancehall album which was rated one of the top 10 reggae albums, and others like them doing the same, then we must perceive that the season is ripe to witness to makers of music. Perceive the times, and grasp the moment.

So, what we need are some CEOs for Project OUT, some Chief Evangelistic Organizers, who have the outward vision and desire to pound the pavement, door to door, street to street, lane to lane, with a message of hope. Launch out into the deep unknown and view new frontiers. Let this outward vision propel us to view what no one has seen before.

It is that outward vision that leads us to view cities and townships as objects of God's ministry. Look out, and have this outward vision that drives us to perceive crime hot spots, climate change, persistent poverty, extortion and exploitation as a basis for ministry. The church's reason for being is to look at others. The Church should always be in the service of others. Lift up your heads and look outward. There are many a people on the outside needing someone to witness to them urgently.

URGENT

Unceasing urgency is characteristic of mission at all times. From the moment of the meeting between Jesus and the Samaritan woman, the whole scene changed. There was no casualness or complacency. Instead, there was an urgency to deal with perceived needs and to offer appropriate answers, with emphasis on possibilities for transformation, now and in the long term.

TWO ● PRESIDENTIAL PROCLAMATIONS

Unfortunately, too many Christians, churches and denominations are in a state of complacency. There is a feeling of satisfaction and contentment with poor achievements. There is a comfort level with the status quo, the dated legacy of former achievements, and average performance. We have become stagnant and stale in our mission work.

Then there is what we want to call activism, which is activity for activity's sake, like a dog chasing its tail. It is movement without a mission. It is zeal without knowledge. It is passion without a purpose. It is fast and furious, but foolish. So, we are like one of the seven churches of Asia Minor, the church at Sardis. The analysis of that church was that "you have a reputation of being alive, but you are dead..." (Rev. 3:1 NIV). We feel good about ourselves and about our reputation for being alive and active, but the truth is that we are deceiving others and just self-indulgent.

While some are complacent and others are busy doing nothing, there are yet others who are simply not urgent in witnessing because they are in a state of spiritual depression; the collective congregation is downcast. A deadness engulfs the spirits of the saints, leaving behind a paralysis of will and sapping the energy of the congregants. We are in that state because we have become overwhelmed by the breadth, depth and height of the many and varied problems we have. We forget the resource of the ever-living presence of Christ. Remember the screaming and scared disciples forgot the power of the presence of Jesus in the boat when they were overwhelmed by the sudden storm on the sea and Jesus was sleeping (Mark 4:35-41). They failed to discern the difference Jesus makes in our lives who calms nature and who has power over diseases, demons and death. When there is spiritual depression, there is no urgency.

So, this morning, February 26, we declare a State of Urgency, because we need to witness with fervency. It is now or never; this opportunity knocks once, and it is a matter of life and death with eternal consequences. By the power of the resurrection, we declare a State of Urgency. Behave with urgency in our witnessing, and our values, attitudes and actions will change, and people will sense it, see it and seize it.

Urgency in our witnessing will lead to at least three things: being prompt, being persistent and being passionate.

Urgency in witnessing is about being prompt. Witness without delay. Be about God's business without hesitation. Witness with urgency to

Witnessing Fervently

children before they reach nine years old. Use the recently launched manual for children "Growing in Faith", which was produced by the JBU under the leadership of Sister Cynthia Anderson. Reach children with the Gospel, and lay a godly foundation from early so that when they grow old, they will not depart from it (Prov. 22:6). Reach them quickly because they grow fast and they learn fast, and we need to get the proper godly values in early. As we share the Gospel with children, remember that they are made in the image and likeness of God with intellect, personality, conscience, mind and emotions. Once we recognize the importance of children, we will move with greater urgency.

Our youths who are unattached, unskilled and underemployed are languishing under difficult conditions and they need the Gospel that satisfies, saves and sustains, and they need it yesterday. It is critical to reach young people with the Gospel promptly because, according to one study, the majority of lasting commitments to a life of Christian discipleship are made by people under the age of 21. On Thursday, a medical doctor told me that for every single university student he sees, a psychologist who has an office besides him sees ten university students. Our brightest and best students have little coping skills. Young people need Jesus promptly.

Then there are women who are facing oppression, contempt, discrimination, and hostility in Jamaica. Offer women healing and hope promptly. Witness to them so that they can experience the joys of being appreciated, celebrated, cherished, respected and loved.

In fact, witness promptly to all persons who are considered to be the lost, the lowest and the least. This challenge is of great importance requiring swift action. Because of the danger and the importance of the mission, it needs attention really soon, before anything else. Give it priority attention now!

Urgency in witnessing must bepersistent. This type of witnessing is unceasing, constant, determined, insistent, and it does not give up easily. It is witnessing without ceasing as we go about our normal, natural business. Wherever we go, we are witnessing. Do not be easily fazed when the results are not what we expected. If at first, we try and do not succeed, then try again: persistence. In 2000, my wife Mary and I went to Orlando to visit Disney World. A salesman was trying to sell us a timeshare, but we declined the offer. He then said to us that for every three persons he tries, one will buy his product. He was not daunted by our refusal. He just went on to someone

TWO ● Presidential Proclamations

else. Oh to God, we would be like that salesman and be fearless in witnessing to others and not be fazed by a 'no' now and then. During the lunch break, lift up your heads from the food, write down three names on your programmes, and intentionally pray for and witness to them for the rest of this year! Think of people you want to see make a commitment to God and pledge to encourage them to attend church, pledge to pray for them and, if the opportunity arises, witness to them fervently. That is our 3 in 1 project.

Urgency in witnessing ought to be passionate. Engage in spreading the good news with great zeal and enthusiasm. We must do it with all our might, strength, body and soul. We must do it with all our emotions and intellect. We need to testify about God as if fire is shut up in our bones, as if our lives depended on it, as if there is nothing more important to do and be.

Lift up your eyes and look outwards, and witness with urgency, letting no hindrance stop the progress in witnessing. Thrust forward, because people are reeling under conviction of the Holy Spirit, ripe for conversion, ready for counselling, and receptive to accepting Christ as Saviour and Lord.

Thrust

Apart from self-preoccupation that prevents the outward look, recurring hindrances in many and different forms become barriers to carrying out the appropriate urgent ministry. What are the hindrances we face in responding promptly, and executing with persistence and passion? Are there irrelevant customs and conventions, or unwillingness to change and try new and different methods? Is there a commitment to seeing and doing things in set ways rather than novel ways? Be like the woman at the well who encountered many hindrances, such as being a woman who was seen as property, as half-bred Jew, the least in society, and inferior in civilization, but she pressed forward and woke the town and told the people that Jesus the Christ was Lord of her history and life.

Follow the example of Jesus who disregarded the age-old turf war between Jews and Samaritans. Jesus changed his plans in view of certain threats that emerged at that moment. We need to be flexible to respond to every threat to witnessing fervently. Thrust against any obstacle and take a cue from the words of Jamaican gospel artiste George Banton (2000), "Give Me Pass, Let Me Praise" ("My Jesus

WITNESSING FERVENTLY

and I/ Give Me Pass, Let Me Praise"). We say to those who have no urgency in witnessing, "Gi mi pass mek mi witness fi mi Jesus."

Away with our made-up hindrances, such as thinking that we do not understand all the doctrines of the faith, or that we need more training to witness. Share our life-changing testimonies and daily testimonies of his grace, mercy, forgiveness and love. It does not need to be systematic; it only needs to be sincere. It does not need to be said with eloquence, but just with enthusiasm. Nobody can tell our history of salvation with God better than we ourselves.

Is there someone here who can testify? Tell them about the life, death and resurrection of Jesus, the hope of the world.

As we thrust forward in witnessing, we ought to trust God for the results. Just be faithful and committed, and leave the outcome to God. Just do the planting and watering, and leave the increase to God. Learn from the life of George Liele who started Baptist witness in Jamaica in 1783. He planted a church in Jamaica, and he faced many man-made obstacles, but he trusted God for the results, and the church grew so fast he had to call for help from overseas. Trust God for the results as we witness fervently.

On Friday, we had an open-air service in Water Square, Falmouth, and while the worship service was going on, there were hindrances, with people playing crown and anchor, checkers, eating, drinking and smoking, and "boy a check a shy girl", but the preacher Revd Davewin Thomas, pastor of Burchell Baptist Church, kept on thrusting. In my walk around the square, I saw a man who seemed under conviction. I introduced myself to him. He said he was Roy from Bottom Town, Trelawny. His wife died in 2006. They have five children. I asked him what he thought about the sermon. He said it was okay. I asked him if he was a Christian. He said no. I asked him whether he had given thought to being a Christian. He said his wife had been a member of Clark's Town Baptist. He said he did not want to make one step, two steps, and then be unable to make the third step. I told Roy that for him and all of us, it is God who has to help us make step one, two, three, and onwards. I then told him: go to Rev. Dr. Vincent Fletcher and tell him that you are ready. I do not know if he will, but I leave the results to God.

Thrust forward ever, backward never, as we witness with urgency and fervency.

CONCLUSION

We have proclaimed Project OUT, that is, Outward Urgent Thrust. We are saying that the Baptist, mentioned in the introduction, who did not witness to her co-worker does not represent the best of us. Instead, we say help is on the way; more witnesses are on their way. We have a host of witnesses who are coming in the power of the resurrection of Jesus. We have people of God who are singing from the same Sankey saying:

> Something down inside of me telling me to go out.
> The Holy Ghost down inside of me telling me to go out, go OUT.

GIVING FREELY

2017 JAMAICA BAPTIST UNION ASSEMBLY

> **Scripture Lesson: Matthew 10:1-10**
>
> *"Heal the sick, cleanse the lepers, raise the dead, cast out demons. Freely you have received, freely give"* (Matt. 10:8 NKJV).

» 22 February 2017

Last year in the 2016 Assembly, as the then president of the JBU Michael Shim-Hue explained the sub-theme "Living the Sacrificial Life", he said among other things "that any life which is to be lived sacrificially must begin with total surrender of that life to God – not surrendering partly, not partial surrender, not periodic surrender, but surrendering continually and completely". Therefore, the task this year is for us to look at five topics emanating from living the sacrificial life: that is, witnessing fervently; serving faithfully; holding firmly; living fully; and giving freely. My privilege and responsibility are to explore "Giving Freely", the topic for this evening's presentation, and we will look at the text in Matthew, chapter 10, and in particular verse 8, where Jesus instructed his disciples to "Heal the sick, raise the dead, cleanse the lepers, cast out demons", and reminded them of the basis for this expectation: "freely ye received, freely give" (ASV).

GIVING FREELY

This verse "Freely you have received; freely give" (NIV) has often been confined to when we are collecting "tithes and offerings", or on fundraising occasions. Such a confinement is a grave limitation imposed on the text. It robs us of the richness of the text, the all-embracing nature of the verse, and the potential and implications for it to be applied to the totality of our lives, and the implications this text has for the totality of our lives as God's people in God's world.

When we fail to give freely, it means that we are going contrary to the intent of the text and the mission will be poorly executed and conditions get worse. We are failing to grasp that our gift giving should fund the mission, relieve genuine need, and execute the mission through time management and appropriate use of knowledge and skills. Instead of pursuing the mission of God, we are chasing after money. In addition, we become self-centred with our time and our talents. This dominant culture against giving freely is outside of the Church, but also within the church. Sad to say, this is an area of great disobedience and default in our Christian practice, much to our own peril under God. Some have no time for God, for God's people, for God's business. When we behave like that, we are going contrary to the intent of God's instructions.

This topic, "Giving Freely", complements this text and emphasizes the quality of the text. To give is to make available, to offer and to present to a receiver what they need. And giving freely means it must be done without force or fear, without reservations and without expecting rewards, not out of duty or under duress, but having such features as being generous, voluntary and spontaneous. This type of giving is what the text commends: it is countercultural, radical and revolutionary giving. It goes against the grain of popular practice. It uproots our prevailing practice. It establishes a different pattern for gift giving. This paradigm shift in gift giving in the church and in the country will result in health over diseases, acceptance over discrimination, life over death, and deliverance from demons. Both the topic and the text complement each other and call for a supernatural giving of self and all that the self possesses.

The context of this text "Freely you have received; freely give" (NIV) places it in the middle of an all-important mission, one presented as being urgent, necessary and important. The urgency of the occasion is communicated by Jesus' act of commissioning the twelve. The necessity of the mission being discharged without unnecessary interference, distraction, diversion or digression due to concerns about

TWO ● PRESIDENTIAL PROCLAMATIONS

personal comfort and personal safety is emphasized. The significant nature of the task to be accomplished is stated: that is, to proclaim the arrival of the kingdom of heaven and to have power over disease, discrimination, death and demons. Accordingly, the fundamental basis, rationale and motivation – the key to the effective pursuit of the mission – are stated: "freely ye received, freely give" (ASV). Today, at this very juncture in our life and history as a church, we are addressed directly with the same mandate of proclaiming the good news of salvation with power. We are facing conditions that bear the same marks of the original context, with people oppressed by diseases, discrimination, by the angel of death going to and fro over the land, by demons and principalities and powers, with the only modification being that there is far greater importance, urgency and intensity with regard to the mission, and potentially even more dangerous outcomes if we fail to execute.

We know the state and conditions of human life as they exist in our world in general and in our context in particular:

- Widening income disparity in the United States, United Kingdom, Haiti and Jamaica
- Persistent poverty in Haiti with a poverty rate of 77 per cent of the population
- High murder rate in Jamaica
- Random criminality in St James
- Sexual abuse and assault of our girls, boys and women
- Poor parenting of our young, including inadequate diet and uninformed moral guidance
- Infectious diseases scaring Caribbean people
- Lethargy in funding and toiling in the mission of God
- Splintering of the one church continues with Jamaica having 600 denominations

Against this backdrop of the urgency of the situation, the gravity of the oppression and the importance of the need, we are called, commanded and commissioned to give freely. We need to heed the word of our Lord, which comes to us with great force and power and authority, to marshal all our God-given resources and put them to use in the mission of liberation and transformation. There can be no delay because delay is danger. This is the moment. This is the time. If we do not make the move, we stand to be held eternally accountable for the distress of our fellow human beings. This mission is challenging, important, serious and urgent. This is no easy task; this is no walk in the park. However, in the spirit of the text itself, we know and are assured that in Jesus, the Christ, and in the Holy Spirit, we are equipped and entrusted with God's most powerful and effective provisions to go all the way with utmost diligence and unwavering commitment.

If this is going to be done, there are some factors that will come into play.

The Defiance we must Exhibit

We are hindered immensely by the practice of giving with strings attached. This must be resisted with every strength we have. We defy with every fibre of our individual and collective being those giving with self-serving calculation; giving with manipulative intention; giving with serious deception; and giving with damaging misrepresentation. Defiance and resistance must be practised all the way and at all times.

Resist those who Resist those who give and ask at the same time: "What is in it for me?" Some give with the expressed intention to boast or to gain a benefit. Some will only give if there is a photo opportunity attached to the giving. So, the giving of a scholarship is not about the scholar primarily but about the giver promoting self. The establishment of some foundations is not primarily to help the less fortunate, but to avoid taxes and parade the company. So, these well heeled and well connected persons give with one hand and take back goods and services with two hands, thereby further enriching the rich and making the poor poorer. Is it therefore any surprise that the gap between persons who are rich and those who are poor is getting wider?

In addition, some men see sex as a natural and necessary transactional commodity and offer to help expecting sexual intercourse in exchange. Trinidadian Singing Sandra in a calypso classic "Die with my Dignity" (2009) relates a story about the difficulty faced by a girl in finding a job. She found a boss man who promise to help: "But when the man let down the condition, nothing else but humiliation, / They want to see you whole anatomy, they want to see what you

TWO ● PRESIDENTIAL PROCLAMATIONS

doctor never see, / They want to do what you husband never do..." This type of giving allows the giver to benefit by grabbing his "pound of flesh", and after this romp and a baby result, the man will not allow his name to be on the child's birth certificate. In fact, he will not give the child a prayer or the mother the time of day. No wonder the society is plagued with many deep-seated problems caused by these deep pocketed persons. Receiving from these rich rogues is risky. Resist these self-absorbed and self-adoring givers.

Be defiant in the face of those who give with manipulative intent. They give, but the receiver is always like a puppet on a string. These so-called godfathers demand from recipients a code of silence, an oath of secrecy and a life of seclusion in light of their corrupt practices. This garrison tactic means the person or community or country is enslaved to the giver and has to do the giver's bidding all the time. Any defiance can cost people their lives. So, it should not baffle us that the murder rate is rising. It has its roots in this type of giving and risky receiving. Be defiant and resist any don, politician, scammer and anyone who gives to create an unwholesome dependence. Resist any country who gives aid to Jamaica, and as a condition we have to support its geopolitical ambition slavishly. Cut those strings.

Be defiant and discerning of those who give with debilitating deception. Know when it is a three-card trick which promises much and delivers next to nothing and extracts more in return.

These givers are claiming that there is no free lunch, that a good or service cannot be received at no cost, save for what it costs the giver! They are devaluing the giving by placing a price tag on that which ought to be priceless. These strings-attached givers fail to understand that a true gift ought to be placed at the disposal of God, and must be left to do what God wills it to do. These strings attached givers can learn from God how to give freely.

THE DYNAMIC WE MUST EMBRACE

The constant complaint of declaring we do not have what it takes to accomplish the task, that is, we have no money, no talent, no technical support, makes God a liar (like saying He does not provide), or makes God seem unreasonable (as if He is giving us a basket to carry water), or makes God look like a tyrant demanding that we engage in a mission which he has not equipped us for. The cry of asking first how much is in the budget, rather than asking whether this undertaking is of the Lord, means that we believe God is either unable or unwilling to supply the resources we need to execute His instructions.

However, the pattern and model we received from the Lord is that He gives beyond all expectations – giving that is never subjected to being exhausted – thereby equipping and empowering us for the mission to overcome or endure disease, discrimination, death, demons and difficulties. We need to embrace the pattern and model of giving freely, which we received freely from God in Christ, and which has been entrusted to us for us to pursue it with the enabling Holy Spirit. This is the effective dynamic with which we must operate.

God the Father's gift for us in Jesus is free for everyone, meaning there is no cost, and therefore no one has any excuse not to accept and receive the gift of salvation and membership in the kingdom of God. It is full and free salvation, so there is no excuse. In addition, God the Father's gift for us in Jesus is for all, meaning it is for everyone, without exception. God's blessings of wholeness and wellness are for all persons. God does not desire that anyone should perish, "but that all should come to repentance" (2 Pet. 3:9 KJV). Salvation is for everyone, no matter his or her past sins – no exception.

The dynamic we must embrace is giving, which is beyond all expectation. God's giving to us is more than asked for, more than we could hope for. Persons went to Jesus or were taken to Jesus for healing of a physical nature, but then they heard also that their sins were forgiven. Jesus said to a paralyzed man, "Son, thy sins be forgiven thee" (Mark 2:5 KJV). The forgiveness of sins is a dimension of human wellness which that man did not expect. We need to embrace giving more than was asked for.

God's gift of grace to us is more than we deserve - just like the experience of the prodigal son. We who were unqualified, unfit, unprepared for the position of ministers of the Gospel are called by God to spread the good news of hope. God calls us and equips us with spiritual gifts to minister to others and engage in a powerful public ministry.

God's gift of grace can never be exhausted. The source is never empty, no matter how many persons access it and how many times it is accessed. There will always be more than enough for everyone, every time. Paul writing to the Corinthians said, "And God is able to make all grace abound toward you; that ye, always having all sufficiency in all things, may abound to every good work..." (2 Cor. 9:8

TWO • PRESIDENTIAL PROCLAMATIONS

KJV). God's gift to us cannot be exhausted. God's gift of eternal life through Jesus is a prime example, in that it is unlimited and unending. Let us join Jabez, Jamaican gospel artiste, and sing from the track "Am Drinking from My Saucer" (2011): "I thank God, for all his blessing on me / And the mercies he's bestowed… / I'm drinking from my saucer, cause my cup has over flown".

Imagine for a moment what Jamaica would look like if we were to embrace and emulate this dynamic of giving, and if our government policy, our company procedure, our church polity, our family practice were all marked by gift giving, wherein the gift is given without exception, and the gift is beyond all expectations, and will never be exhausted. That would be a New World Order of Giving. Guess what! This type of gift giving is the giving that will "heal the sick, raise the dead, cleanse the lepers, cast out demons" (Mark 10:8 ASV). Embrace it and emulate it! Based on what God in Christ has done for us and entrusted us to do likewise by the power of the Spirit, then by similarly giving freely, we who are now different because we have accepted God's gift of grace, should make a difference.

THE DIFFERENCE WE MUST EXECUTE

As a people and a nation, we must recognize that things cannot continue to be as they have always been. The society is in need of serious reordering and reengineering if it hopes to avoid descending into further disorder and decadence of the most disastrous proportions. The government and also various civil society institutions, such as lobby groups and religious organizations, have been aware of this and are making responses meant to make a difference for better. For example, there is the major thrust by the government referred to as the growth agenda. Nevertheless, it appears as if there is a lack of a moral agenda, a moral vision and moral values. This lack facilitates the murder and mayhem, and the lawlessness and vigilante justice. To the best of our knowledge, there is no companion moral agenda to the growth agenda that has equal prominence, has a strategic plan, is adequately resourced and with personnel to see to its oversight. But we need a consensus moral agenda, moral vision, and moral values which are just, responsible, sustainable and wholesome in order to flourish. They would provide the motive and nature of our goal for a better Jamaica.

What would this moral agenda entail and possibly look like? There are seven principles we could depend on:

- Value all human life
- Value the totality of life
- Zero tolerance of corruption and sexual assault
- Enforcement of the legitimate laws
- Equality of all under the law
- Encourage solidarity and simplicity of lifestyle
- Access to the basic goods and services, opportunities and resources needed for all to live in decency and die with dignity

This is where the collective church comes in, with our moral legacy informed by our religious tradition and folk wisdom, to produce policies and actions committed to the cause of the common good. We cannot see prosperity only in economic terms, but prosperity ought to be a means to live well and to live within our means, to live well with each other, and to live well with the natural environment.

This is not a call to Baptists only but to all who belong to the household of faith. Based on the prayer of Jesus, "that all of them may be one" (John 17:21 NIV), then this understanding will inspire us to work together and be the primary missional motivation for the joint witness and work undertaken by the denominations. The task is too great, the task is too necessary, the task is too important and too urgent for Baptists alone, so let us people of goodwill, especially of the community of faith, join hands together in a partnership marked by mutuality, equality and solidarity. We need all hands on board to give freely for this mission with our time, our witness, our skill, our talent, our knowledge and, yea, our total selves. We need to come together and proclaim the good news that through Jesus' death and resurrection the principalities and powers have already been disgraced, disarmed and defeated; God reigns over disease, discrimination, death and demon possession. This is the full gospel, which is the power of God unto salvation. Make a difference by exposing, naming, shaming and challenging that which would defy or deny the possibilities of the abundant life. Expose deception, expose oppression, expose exploitation, whether outside the church or within the church.

However, proclamation cannot be confined to preaching from a pulpit. It also involves Christian education, taking time to disciple people, and enabling them to disciple others, and it involves all

TWO ● PRESIDENTIAL PROCLAMATIONS

making ethical choices and discerning right from wrong. Proclamation of the Gospel means being involved in community and country through social action and social justice. We must be emancipation loving, justice seeking believers, based on the value of equality of all and justice for all. We need to declare a message of liberation. This means we have to engage in advocacy. We need to advocate on behalf of persons who are lost, left out, left behind and considered losers, and become the voice of the voiceless.

> To dons of garrison communities that hold people to a code of silence and an oath of secrecy and a life of seclusion – "Thus saith the Lord... Let my people go..." (Exod. 9:1 KJV).

> To powerful people who charge high fees, unconscionable taxes and unreasonable tithing – "Thus saith the Lord... Let my people go..."

> To a society which has allowed and cooperated with 500,000 persons in squatter communities which are not organized and lack adequate institutional support – "Thus saith the Lord... Let my people go..."

> To the Israeli government, which is an occupying power over the Palestinians, who live under inhumane conditions in Gaza, the West Bank and East Jerusalem – "Thus saith the Lord... Let my people go..."

Furthermore, we say:
- Celebrate informers who report criminal acts – Lift them up.
- Applaud sanitation workers who work so that our environment can be healthy – Lift them up.
- Honour those who work with persons who are diseased, dying and facing discrimination – Lift them up.
- Praise warders who live and work in the maximum security prison facilitates that are inhumane – Lift them up.
- Pray for those who live and work in areas where the air quality is awful – Lift them up.
- Honour those who enhance worship and witness, such as our musicians – Lift them up.

Giving Freely

And for:

- Victims of violent crime and those whose loved ones were brutally killed – Show them Love.
- Victims of sexual assault, physical and emotional abuse – Show them Love.
- Pregnant women and persons with disabilities who get J$1,200 a fortnight on the PATH programme – Show them Love.
- Persons who do not earn a livable wage and lack the necessities of life – Show them Love.
- Children who do not have their fathers' names on their birth certificates, and who do not know their fathers – Show them Love.
- People who need a pint of blood to live – Show them Love.

This liberation, this emancipation, this letting go of oppressed people, the lifting up of the genuine workers, loving the persons who are exploited, vulnerable and weak, will all lead to transformative engagement. To effect this type of change, the change agent must engage in absolute selflessness. Then, the change agent and the change become one. We are the change. Then, the messenger and the message become one. We are the message. Then, we become truly one with God.

What does it mean to act with absolute selflessness? It means, among other things, recognizing that the authority and power to engage in ministry has been freely given to you and received by you, so give freely to others. Acting with absolute selflessness means to commit to living the sacrificial life by embracing freely a life of self-denial, which will make our lives and our gifts available to serve God's purposes in the world.

Additionally, it leads to witnessing fervently, giving freely, serving faithfully, holding firmly and living fully, individually and collectively:

(a) Without constraints

(b) Without counting the cost

(c) Without calling for a compensation

(d) Without comparing our contribution

TWO ● Presidential Proclamations

(e) Without concluding that our contribution is ever equal to what God deserves

That is how we will make a difference: by promoting morality based on the value of life and the value of the totality of life; by preaching the good news with power; by understanding that God grants victory over diseases, discrimination, death and demons. This preaching of the Gospel also includes proclaiming advocacy on behalf of the voiceless. Finally, we make a difference by portraying absolute selflessness.

We made a difference in the past when Paul Bogle and George William Gordon, Native Baptist leaders, now national heroes, propelled by a mission-charge, established churches, Negro settlements and schools, which also spurred church development and wholistic growth.

We are engaged in ministry through the Salt Spring Peace and Justice Centre, St James, enabling peace in surrounding communities. On Friday, we will launch our blood drive. On Sunday, we recognize sanitation workers. Every day, the Gospel is preached with power; every day we are encouraged to minister to the needy. Next month, we launch the Castor Bean project, and we are part of the restoration ministry in Haiti.

Conclusion

Much more work needs to be done. Therefore, let the Christian community engage in effective management in practical actions and deliberate interventions that will result in fundamental and radical change for the good of the people, so that Jamaica, Haiti, the Caribbean and the world can become a wholesome place, a righteous place where we can all live, work, raise families, do business, study and worship God. Amen.

Commitment

Let open hands be the image representing our gift giving where blessings enter and exit; where we get in order to give; where we are helped to help others. The call is for us to become a more giving church and country. Please join me and stand with your hands outstretched as a sign of commitment to giving freely as we say together:

GIVING FREELY

Mary Maxwell's song "Channels Only" (1900): "Channels only, blessed Master, / But with all Thy wondrous pow'r / Flowing through us, Thou canst use us / Every day and every hour."

Give, Give, Give!

THREE
SPECIAL OCCASION SERMONS

NEUTRAL ON NOTHING
DERRICK SADDLER'S ORDINATION

Scripture Lesson: Luke 4:18-20

"The Spirit of the Lord is on me, because he has anointed me to proclaim good news to the poor. He has sent me to proclaim freedom for the prisoners and recovery of sight for the blind, to set the oppressed free, to proclaim the year of the Lord's favour" (Luke 4:18-19 NIV).

» *5 September 2019*

Recently, a former US Ambassador to Jamaica, Pamela Bridgewater, gave me a book entitled *Neutral on Nothing*. The book tells the story of her grandfather, Revd B.H. Hester, pastor of Shiloh Baptist Church, Fredericksburg, Virginia, who stood up for justice against the odds in a racist, white supremacist United States. This slim biography has a title I want to borrow as the title for this sermon, "Neutral on Nothing". The word to pastor and people is "Neutral on Nothing". The word to those who occupy the pulpit or the pew is "Neutral on Nothing".

Jesus quoted from the prophetic tradition of Isaiah, who was neutral on nothing. Jesus picked up the mantle of the prophet Isaiah who said, "Is not this the kind of fasting I have chosen: to loose the chains of injustice and untie the cords of the yoke, to set the oppressed free and break every yoke?" (58:6 NIV), and "The Spirit of the Sovereign

LORD is on me, because the LORD has anointed me to proclaim good news to the poor. He has sent me to bind up the brokenhearted, to proclaim freedom for the captives and release from darkness for the prisoners" (61:1 NIV). Both Jesus and Isaiah were neutral on nothing.

Jesus at the start of his public ministry identified with the outcast, the exploited and the marginalized, not the supposedly wise, wealthy and well connected. Jesus was not neutral on the issue of freedom, believing that the enslaved would be set free. Jesus was not neutral on the issue of forgiveness of financial debts and sins. Jesus was not neutral on the need for rest, whether for humans, animals or crops. When the disciples saw the thousands of hungry people, the disciples wanted to send them away, but Jesus refused to be neutral, and he said that they had a right to daily food, and so he fed them. The Pharisees said, "Do not heal a human being on the Sabbath, but on the Sabbath, you can rescue the sheep." Jesus said no. Jesus affirmed that humans are more worthy than birds, pets, dogs, sparrows and sheep (Matt. 10:31, 6:26). Jesus was not neutral on the right to health care for the ill, sick and diseased people.

The life of Jesus was the life of someone who was neutral on nothing. Hence, he was always at loggerheads with the religious establishment over the Sabbath. Jesus was at odds with the political structure with its oppressive taxation. Jesus confronted the principalities and powers that kept the people in bondage. Jesus bucked the trend of traditionalism and said he was the new way. Perhaps the statement that crystalizes the idea that Jesus was neutral on nothing is the statement: "You have heard that it was said... But I say to you..." (Matt. 5:21-22 NKJV). Jesus inaugurated a new covenant, a New Testament.

Derrick, and people of God, you cannot be neutral on the issue of fallowing, freedom, food, forgiveness and fasting. There is no place to be neutral. Once you choose one side, you are automatically opposed by the other side. Either you are going to serve God, or you going to serve Mammon. Either you are going to execute God's ministry, or you are going follow the dictates of Satan and his surrogates.

HAVE A CONVICTION

Have a settled position: have a firmly held position, persuasion, belief or opinion, based on your interpretation of the Bible and your understanding of God. Have a conviction which is nurtured through prayer

THREE ○ SPECIAL OCCASION SERMONS

and your experience with the Holy Spirit, and observed through the wonders of nature and the environment.

Having a conviction is not stubbornness or pigheadness. To have a conviction is not to be dogmatic or unwilling to listen; it is not refusing to be open to learning new, different and better ideas, even in the face of compelling arguments or reasons. Having a conviction is having a settled position until better comes.

Some of us have strong convictions, and no one knows; they are safely hidden in the heart. We play it safe with our deeply held beliefs. Our philosophy is "cowad man kip soun bone". Only a few close friends know our true convictions. However, we need to stand by our convictions. We have too many church leaders who lack moral fortitude. You know the story of the likeable, competent and caring pastor in rural Jamaica. There was a couple having marital problems, and the wife visited the manse and explained her position, and then the pastor concluded without hearing the other side, and told the wife, "You right, you right". A few hours after, the husband visited the manse, and he outlined his side of the story, and the pastor said to him, "You right, you right." Unbeknownst to all, the pastor's wife was overhearing all these conversations. She tackled her husband and asked him how come when the wife came, he said to her, "You right, you right," and then when the husband came with a completely opposite story to the wife's you told him, "You right, you right." The pastor's wife said, "You are a hypocrite," and the pastor responded by saying, "You right, you right." This pastor had no backbone. He was trying to please everybody. He had no conviction. Have a conviction, a settled position based on expertise and experience with God, as revealed in Jesus, the Christ. When we sit on the fence, both sides suspect us. When we are neither fish nor fowl, people do not know where we stand. When there are persons who are enslaved, heartbroken, impoverished and lacking a future, then we have to take sides.

In addition, we cannot "sidung pon cow back an cuss cow skin". You cannot sit on the back of a cow and curse the skin of the cow. You cannot be getting a free ride from the oppressor, and while enjoying the ride, you are cursing him. So, we cannot be in the pocket of the oppressor, and turn around and "cuss" the oppressor.

You cannot be a Spanish machete which cuts both ways. You cannot ride two horses at same time, trying to be friends with both sides. You either with '1 Peter' or '2 Peter.', those two People's National Party

(PNP) politicians who are vying for the presidency of the party. You either with Dr Peter Phillips or Peter Bunting.

According to one of the most quotable speakers of the 20th century, Baptist minister and US civil rights activist Revd Dr Martin Luther King Jr., "The ultimate measure of a man is not where he stands in moments of comfort and convenience, but where he stands in times of challenge and controversy. The true neighbor will risk his position, his prestige, and even his life for the welfare of others" (*Strength of Love* 1963). Have strong convictions in moments of challenge and controversy.

What will help us to develop strong, firm and settled convictions? Know the word of God. Jesus knew the word of God, so it affected his behaviour and ministry, and helped him to overcome temptations and to do the will of God. Derrick, know the word of God. People of God, read the word of God. Enjoy reading scriptures, not just a text, but a chapter a day. Study to show thyself approved (2 Tim. 2:15), rightly interpreting scriptures for the times, and in order to gain a proper understanding of the ways and will of God. Study so that you speak with authority, having been to the throne of God, and having listened to the counsels of God. Then, you will be faithful to the apostles' teaching, and you will not be swayed by these "hurry come up" apostles, many of whom are mere charlatans. Be a skilled student of the word of God, so that you can preach in and out of season. Study to know what to preach, what to do and where to go in ministry. Know the word of God, not for uncritical acceptance of dogmas, doctrines and cultural absolutes, but rather for a knowledge of the word of God that facilitates understanding, reflection and participation in decision making, and sharing in shaping a godly society.

Know the world. Know your environment. Recognize that we are in a gospel hostile environment, both outside the church and inside the church. The church no longer has the status it once had. And when we are in a dominant position, do not misuse it to crush minorities. Do rigorous research, adept analysis, proper planning, insightful implementation, and extensive evaluation in assessing the ministry God has assigned to you. Be able to identify trends and fashion that are designed to re-enslave God's people. Watch what is happening around you. In addition, know the ways of the worldly system; know the tricks of the devil and the pitfalls of Satan. Understand how the principalities and powers are operating in our community, our country and the world.

Then having done all, take a preferential option for the poor. Follow the advice of Baptist scholar Burchell Taylor and ensure that the "church taking sides". Be engaged in affirmative action for the disadvantaged, dispossessed and depressed, so that they too will be treated fairly and will have access to goods and services to help them live a life of dignity. Have a conviction in your preaching, teaching and training, and take sides; have a conviction, and in your praying and singing, take sides; in your going out and coming in, take sides. Be neutral on nothing.

BE COMPASSIONATE

We cannot be indifferent and emotionless concerning the plight of persons who are poor, abused and exploited. Being compassionate is not pitying people and seeing them as hangers-on befitting of receiving handouts and "hand-me-downs" only. Such attitudes rob people, made in the image and likeness of God, of their dignity and turn people into mendicants dependent on politicians, pastors, drug dealers and dons.

We cannot be indifferent and emotionless concerning the plight of persons who are poor, abused and exploited. Being compassionate is not pitying people and seeing them as hangers-on befitting of receiving handouts and hand-me-downs only. Such attitudes rob people, made in the image and likeness of God, of their dignity and turn people into mendicants dependent on politicians, pastors, drug dealers and dons.

Garnett Roper in his book, *This is the Year of Jubilee*, declared the acceptable year of the Lord the same as declaring the Year of Jubilee. Jesus was the embodiment of Jubilee, the one who ushered in the acceptable year of the Lord, the one who sustains and reinterprets the Jubilee. When prisoners are set free, it is jubilation time. When the blind can see, it is celebration time. When the brokenhearted experience healing, it is time to dance and shout. We cannot experience God's goodness, greatness and graciousness without bursting out into celebration. "Celebrate Jesus, celebrate." We are happy in the Lord.

Your ordination ought to be a time of celebration, because you are ushering in a ministry that is based on biblical convictions, and you will be compassionate, and you will do something about the conditions of the people who are weary, weak, weeping and worried.

Fasting, according to the prophet Isaiah, is not refraining and abstaining from food only, but also hungering and thirsting after righteousness and justice. Fasting is also abstinence from all forms of oppression. Fasting is not about refraining from eating only, but also about feeling compassion towards the destitute. In Jesus' mission statement, Jesus not only quotes Isaiah 61 but also adds Isaiah 58, because his mission was to link fasting with social responsibility.

Fasting is a time for celebration of the oppressed. Therefore, even fasting is a time of celebration. When the good news is proclaimed to people who are poor, it is celebration time; every time the oppressed are set free, it is celebration time; every time you proclaim the year of the Lord's favour, it is celebration time. When I think of the goodness of Jesus and what he has done for me, my soul cries out "Hallelujah!"

Conclusion

As Frances Havergal, British hymn writer, asked and proclaimed:

> Who is on the Lord's side?
> Who will serve the King? [...]
> We are on the Lord's side –
> Saviour, we are Thine [...]
> Always on the Lord's side –
> Saviour, always Thine!
>
> (*The Baptist Hymn Book* 1962, #534)

We are on the Lord's side, and therefore we the church "taking sides", will be neutral on nothing. Our mission will be marked by a preferential option for people who are poor, oppressed, enslaved, heartbroken and blind.

THREE ● SPECIAL OCCASION SERMONS

Figure 4. Derrick Saddler, Ordinand (*right*), and Devon Dick, Preacher at Ordination Service, Moses Baker Baptist Church, St Thomas

Photograph by Marva Lambert, Member, Boulevard Baptist Church (5 September 2019)

Do the Right Thing
JTA 55ᵀᴴ ANNIVERSARY

> Scripture Lessons: Micah 6:1-8; Luke 12:51-53
> *"He has shown you, O mortal, what is good. And what does the Lord require of you? To act justly and to love mercy and to walk humbly with your God"* (Mic. 6:8 NIV).

» *18 August 2019*

What does the Lord require of thee? Act justly, love mercy and walk humbly with God. In a word, do the right thing. These profound words coming from the mouth of a minor prophet has major significance. It is a statement about doing the right thing so that there can be a compassionate community and a wholesome world. It is a mandate for right living. It is a command for right relationships. Without this foundation, a society descends into anarchy, boredom, boorishness and banality, lacking in originality and innovation. Life becomes a daily grind, marked by mundaneness, mayhem and murders.

Micah calls us to reflect on how to empower people, how to build a society, and the key words are humility, justice and mercy. So, what does God desire and demand? He desires and demands that we act justly, love mercy and walk humbly with him. Above all else, what does God ask for and appeal for? He wants us to affirm justice, be humble and cry for mercy.

Walk Humbly with God – Be Humble

Humility is acting modestly in the presence of God. It is being in agreement with God through constant communion with God. We are urged to be humble. As Paul puts it, "Do not think of yourself more highly than you ought, but rather think of yourself with sober judgment" (Rom. 12:3 NIV). In order to be humble, we need to get rid of inflated notions of ourselves, our class, our church, our political party, our school, our association, our neighbourhood, our type.

Three ● Special Occasion Sermons

Being arrogant, knowing it all, being boastful and full of self-importance, and being dogmatic, always right, are all signs that we lack humility. If we lack humility, it means that we are not walking with God, but rather flying in the face of God. So, formerly, preachers would say "Thus saith the Lord", but nowadays some are so full of ego they say "I decree and declare", playing God.

On July 14, Rayon Simpson, a teacher, in a letter to *The Gleaner*, accused the teaching profession of "squaddie mentality" in seeing no evil and saying nothing in spite of a litany of serious defects in a former minister of education, or even refusing to call for a former head of a tertiary institution to step back for a while. I saw no response from the JTA, not even to say we are working, working, working behind the scenes. Look at St Paul in 1 Corinthians responding to the queries and questions of the people. Be humble and look at the other side, and respond to people. How do we rate ourselves in light of humility?

Additionally, be humble by being teachable. Automation is part of the world and we have to change. When we go to the airport now, many things are automated. There are fewer workers in cane cutting and mixing cement because of automation. We have to be teachable and allow the Holy Spirit to guide us. There are benefits of the technology for all, because of affordability of the Internet and the reach of the Internet, for instance. Be humble and be teachable and use technology to innovate. We have to learn new tricks and techniques. We have to be adaptable.

In addition, remember "humble calf suck di most milk". The humble calf is easily satisfied and grateful with the milk from the cow, while the arrogant calf is greedy, always wanting more than is necessary or needed, and never satisfied; "dem belly never full" and they are never willing to allow other calves to get a suck. When we are humble before God and walk with God, then we are contented, satisfied and fulfilled with what God provides. Be humble and be satisfied with God and His provision.

Act Justly, Affirm Justice

Justice is about treating people fairly and equally, at the basic level, all the time and under all circumstances. To act justly and affirm justice is to recognize that persons who are poor due to the system of exploitation, or due to injustice, a lack of education and skill, and abuse, all have rights to food and freedoms. Justice is not a favour or

DO THE RIGHT THING

privilege extended to persons who lack. Justice is a right and an entitlement for persons who are deprived. Justice is not about handouts which victimize the victims further, strip them of their God-given dignity, and make them mendicants, always dependent.

Justice therefore describes the right to food as being the prerogative of persons who are poor. Prov. 31:8-9 states: "Speak up for those who cannot speak for themselves, for the rights of all who are destitute. Speak up and judge fairly; defend the rights of the poor and needy" (NIV).

What verses! When we go to Proverbs 31, we often start at verse 10 to read about a virtuous woman, but we ignore verses 8 and 9. "Yes now, Spanish Town!" When last did we speak up for those who cannot speak for themselves. Stacey Abrams, first Black female nominee for the post of Governor of Georgia, USA, said last week at Progressive National Baptist Convention Freedom Banquet that silence is not an option and stoicism is not a possibility. We cannot be indifferent and emotionless concerning the plight of persons who are poor. We must speak up and out and call for justice.

Our understanding of peace is often this: no confrontation, no conflict, no controversy, no counterargument and no challenge to leadership. This warped understanding of peace is heard when people say: for a peaceful life, there should be no deliberation, no discussion and no debate; just "trust me". That is paternalism – the policy or practice on the part of people in authority of restricting the freedom and responsibilities of those subordinate to them and dependent on them. That concept of peace breeds injustices.

Acting justly and affirming justice means being a voice for the voiceless; defending the defenceless; and protecting the penniless.

And why do we defend the persons who are poor? Because God does that. Psalm 109:21-22 states, "But you, O Lord my Lord, act on my behalf for your name's sake; because your steadfast love is good, deliver me. For I am poor and needy" (NRSV).

Persons who are poor, in the name of justice, have a right to FOOD, daily food. When Jesus saw the thousands hungry, he did not send them away, but fed them with bread and fish. Hungry people have a right to manna.

Recently, Senator Damion Crawford made a profound point when he said that when you see a security guard with a dog, you can easily note that the dog gets better treatment than the guard. The security guard eats once a day, while his security dog eats three meals a day.

THREE ● SPECIAL OCCASION SERMONS

Dogs are more valuable than humans and are getting better treatment than some people. This is not an option for the Christian. We are always on the side of humans, especially the needy, hungry and poor.

Very often, the rich, powerful and influential people "box bread" out of the mouths of persons who are poor. In the United States, there is a move afoot for action against legal immigrants who benefit from food aid or housing benefits for more than a year. In the United Kingdom, there are persons who are dying from starvation. In 2013, David Clapson, a former soldier, died due to a lack of money for food and medicine. The autopsy showed that his stomach was empty. A few weeks earlier, a job centre had cut off his benefits for not searching hard enough for work. In 2009, the Trussell Trust, the largest food bank network in the United Kingdom, fed 41,000 people, and this year they have fed ten times more people. This state of affairs in the UK is because of government policy and the action of cutting social benefits.

And what about our beloved nation? Maziki Thame, political scientist, and Camilo Thame, business analyst writing in today's *Gleaner* under the caption "Porsches, Poverty, Prosperity" said that the average inflation rate between 2007 and 2017, a ten-year period, was 127 per cent. The minimum wage in 2017 is in effect a reduction by 15 per cent in real purchasing power over 2007 (page G4). These people below the poverty line have rights. A hungry man cannot stand up. A hungry child will have no "pep" in their step.

The Pharisees said: do not heal a human being on the Sabbath, but on the Sabbath, you can rescue the sheep. Why? The sheep was their livelihood and considered more important than people. Humans were less valuable than animals, and therefore expendable. Jesus affirms that humans are more worthy than birds, sparrow and sheep (Matt. 12:11-12, Matt. 10:31, 6:26). The people who are poor have a right to health. Friday's *Daily Observer* reported the junior doctors as saying that because of the lack of equipment and relevant staff, patients die every week. We all know that, but do we care to speak up and speak out on behalf of the rights of those who are destitute and sick?

Justice demands that we also respect religious freedom. The right to religious freedom is the very foundation of all other rights, since relationship with God is at the basis of all life. John Locke (1632-1704), foremost philosopher and political theorist, said in *A Letter Concerning Toleration* (1689) that "all churches [should]... teach that liberty of conscience is every man's natural right... and that nobody ought to be compelled in matters of religion either by law or force". There is a right to worship God based on conscience. We should never criminalize belief in Voodoo, Obeah, atheism, Mormonism, Hinduism or even astrology. I do not believe in any of them, but everybody ought to have a right to their belief.

This country has had a history of martial law which deprived our forebears of their rights. People have a right to freedoms and, according to the Jamaica Charter of Fundamental Rights and Freedoms (Constitutional Amendment) Act, 2011, there should be freedom of movement, freedom of peaceful assembly and association, freedom of expression, freedom of thought and belief and conscience, and the right to protection from search of person and property. Let no one abrogate, abridge or infringe on these rights.

Justice is a value which we are called to establish, demonstrate and affirm. Our watchword should be justice for everyone, every time and everywhere.

LOVE MERCY, CRY FOR MERCY

Whereas justice is to get what we deserve and what we are entitled to, mercy is to get more than we deserve, more than we ask for, and more than we worked for. Jesus gives us more than we deserve in abundance. We get many blessings which we do not deserve. God grants mercies to the just and the unjust.

Mercy is to give someone a jump-start in life.

But who are the ones who get the breaks and the scholarships? Sometimes, it is the bright ones who do not need it. Who get the waivers and the debt write-offs? The genetically connected, the haves, and the high fliers get them. However, mercy is not for those who think they are self-sufficient and self-made; mercy is not for the proud and powerful. It is for persons who are the victims, the voiceless and the vulnerable, those who need a head start in life. That is why as Boulevard Baptist Church celebrates 50 years of ministry as a congregation, we offer medical services, skills training, thrift shop and soup kitchen services, and scholarships to those in need.

It is mercy why some of "we reach where we reach". Some might say "is because they had a godfather why dem reach where dem reach". Others of us will simply say we had God as our Father who pardoned us; who provided for us; who protected us. Nineteen years ago, I was going to speak at the Airy Castle Primary graduation. My mother was with me. I was driving from Kingston to St Thomas, and I felt tired, so I stopped in Yallahs and washed my face. By the time I reached Morant Bay, I fell asleep at the steering wheel and crashed into a parked vehicle. I awoke on the sound of the crash to hear two ladies who were near the parked vehicle cry out, "Look how the man nearly knock we down and kill we!" Can you imagine me being charged for manslaughter? My life would have been different. The mercy of God is why I am here this morning.

When I think of the goodness and graciousness of Jesus, and all that he has done for me, I shout 'Hallelujah!'

The same mercy God extended to us is the same mercy we should extend to the needy. Without mercy we cannot live; without mercy we cannot survive. In the name of mercy, we are to rescue those who are perishing, and be compassionate to those who are dying.

Walk with God and partner with people of faith and goodwill to help those who have been duped, drugged and dumped. Some are in the depths of despair and need mercy. Some are victims of unfairness and suffering and need God's mercy. Have mercy.

Conclusion

Do what is right. It is a commitment to establish, maintain and affirm justice, humility and mercy as foundational to a wholesome society. Do the right thing and "act justly… love mercy and… walk humbly with God" (Mic. 6:8 NIV).

Figure 5. Congregation at Boulevard Baptist for the 60th Anniversary of the JTA Co-operative Credit Union

Photograph by Sebastian Foster of the JTA (20 January 2019)

THREE ● SPECIAL OCCASION SERMONS

EAT WITH SINNERS

JTA CO-OPERATIVE CREDIT UNION 60TH ANNIVERSARY

> Scripture Lessons: Psalm 100, Luke 15:1-2,
> Hebrews 11:1-3, 23-30
> *"This man welcomes sinners and eats with them."*
> *(Luke 15:2 NIV)*

» *20 January 2019*

The implication of the position of the detractors was that Pharisees thought Jesus was a sinner like those he ate with. The detractors said Jesus was a lawbreaker because he healed on the Sabbath (Mark 3:1-6). He was a devil because he cast out demons (Matt. 12:24). He was a low-class sinner because he ate with sinners. When Jesus welcomed and ate with sinners – tax collectors, fraudsters, oppressors – the Pharisees criticized him.

You see, Pharisees, this Jewish sect, were distinctive, meaning they embraced a feeling of superiority. They did not mix with ordinary folks because they felt they were superior to others, that they were more than others, because they claimed they knew the law, rules and regulations better than others. They were self-righteous (Luke 5:31). Their mantra would be, at all cost, do not be seen with sinners, and definitely do not eat with sinners.

Pharisees were powerful, influential, and they could make life difficult for others. In the case of Jesus, they were instrumental in having Jesus crucified. The Pharisees grumbled, complained and murmured greatly, constantly and consistently. They were worried about the ease of access the sinners had to Jesus. They were startled and shocked that the Saviour stopped and stayed with sinners, because to have company with, and to take food in company with, someone was a serious business. As the saying goes, "Show me your company, and I'll tell you who you are." Old-time people would say, "Birds of a feather flock together." Indeed, people of similar interests, ideas and thinking will hang out with each other.

EAT WITH SINNERS

It was true denotatively that Jesus welcomed and ate with sinners, but connotatively the real allegation was that he was one of them – ungodly and a sinner. However, Jesus was fearless in carrying out the mission of God; he welcomed sinners as a sign of his friendship with sinners, and he ate with them in order that sinners would experience empowering fellowship.

That which Jesus was criticized for was his commission to have communion with people of low character.

That which he was maligned for was his mandate to mix with the misfits.

That which he was ridiculed for was his reason for being: to have a relationship with people considered rebels and those revelling in riotous living.

Jesus declared his hand by the type of persons he welcomed and ate with. Jesus was earnest in bringing sinners home. That was his mission, mandate and message.

EMBRACE FEARLESSNESS

Embrace fearlessness in spite of unfair criticism. Be courageous and risk your reputation, risk popularity, for God's sake. Be fearless even when misunderstood, misrepresented and maligned. Do not stop doing God's will, even in the face of innuendoes and half-truths about us and your organization. How many strangers hate us because of how someone else described us? It is a part of life that people who do not know you will say all manner of evil about you, but be fearless in spite of those utterances. Get over unfair criticism.

There are haters, tear-down artists and hostile forces. Bob Marley, reggae icon, in the song "Who the Cap Fit" (1970) sang that your best friend could be your worst enemy because "some will eat and drink with you, then behind them su-su pon you". These lyrics were written after Marley was betrayed. People can really be "bad mind".

Be fearless and boldly go where no one has gone before. Be bold and create a path and leave your footprints. Be a pioneer and leave a legacy. On 9 February 1969, fifty years ago, Revd Luther Gibbs and 31 members started Boulevard Baptist Church. What is the next leap of faith for this church? Establish targets, objectives and goals for 2019. Start something. Challenge ourselves. Learn from persons wiser than ourselves in a particular field. Be inspired by God.

THREE ◉ SPECIAL OCCASION SERMONS

Some 30-odd years ago, I led the members of Fletcher's Grove Baptist Church, Sandy Bay, Hanover, to start a jail ministry at the jail not even 20 metres away. I had no training, no experience and no expertise in jail ministry. I just saw a need and remembered the biblical injunction to visit those who are imprisoned. Therefore, let us see a need, and just do something about it.

Why did the Festival of Choirs start in February 2010? It was because Boulevard Baptist Church had her Anniversary Worship Service in February 2009 to mark 40 years of witness and work and Hanover Street Baptist, our "mother church", was inadvertently not invited. To save face, I realized we needed a closing event of significance, which would be available and affordable for all. The idea and name came in a moment of inspiration – "Festival of Choirs". Prior to that I had never been to a "Festival of Choirs". No one could have predicted that the "Festival of Choirs" would have lasted ten years. However, it has become a feast of music, and many Christians within and outside of the Baptist denomination look forward to it every first Sunday afternoon in February. This "Festival of Choirs" shows that we need to be bold and turn a crisis into a beautiful opportunity.

In 1959, the JTA Co-op Credit Union started from the resolution of teacher W.S.A. Johnson and principal D.C. Gascoigne that it would be the largest credit union in Jamaica. Gascoigne was fearless and launched out in the deep. Go and do likewise.

Extend a Hand of Friendship

Who is a friend? One who wishes the best for you, wants the best for you and works in order that you might be the best you can be, do the best you can, and experience the best that there is on offer.

There are some persons who have friends and make friends in order to monetize the friendship; friendship is an opportunity to make money. Some make friends to enhance their status by being able to say "I know that person". Some make friends in order to have access to the corridors of power. Some make friends in order to win support for a cause. Sometimes, even countries do that. They make friends for economic or geopolitical reasons. However, we ought to make friends to encourage persons to be their best selves. Therefore, engage in friendship evangelism. Friendship evangelism occurs when you become friends with someone, and because you are friends, one of the things you desire is that your friend become a Christian and enjoy the blessings of the Christian life.

Furthermore, extend a hand of friendship by identifying with the person's condition and accepting the person just as he or she is, even while we hope for a better condition and situation for the person. Therefore, care for persons with special needs, not doing it because someday we will need them to help; do it even if they never return the favour. Be a friend because it is the right thing to do. Be a friend because it is a good thing. Jesus healed ten lepers and only one, 10 per cent, returned to say thanks.

Name a miserable, difficult person and I will show you someone who needs a friend. Help even the ungrateful and those who might not even appreciate what we do. Cultivate friendship, invest in friends and value friendships. Spend quality time with friends, which means eating with them, and getting to know them and their needs.

Empowering Fellowship

Fellowship speaks to our relatedness and relationships because of Jesus. It is about sharing in the blessedness of salvation in its fullest. It is a sharing also of the supernatural life of God. Through Jesus' death he brought into being a new creation and a new order. Fellowship with Jesus is also sharing in his sufferings.

Fellowship is also about generous sharing. It is about mutual obligation. It speaks to partnership, participation and involvement in the life of others. Fellowship is about recognizing the equality of all and being in solidarity with all.

Therefore, there is no place for feeling superior and self-righteous in genuine fellowship. Fellowship is not about creating a dependence or giving handouts only. Fellowship is transformational and difference-making. In a fellowship setting, everybody is respected, gifted and contributes.

Eating with the corrupt is not a sign of commending their lifestyle, but it is to recognize that they can be better than they are; it is to acknowledge there is better in them. It is to recognize that the best is yet to come. An intervention for good in a life is empowering.

Eating with sinners is also about eating with those sinned against. Fellowship has to do with sharing in the good times and bad times; the thrills and spills; and the trials and triumphs of those who have been sinned against. It is empowering them to serve God. Moses chose his people over Pharaoh's family, although he benefitted from being in Pharaoh's family by having access to good education and good facilities. Moses turned his back on fame and fortune in order to be in solidarity with his national, people who were oppressed, dispossessed and exploited. That ought also to be our mission, ministry and mandate. Therefore, love empowering persons who have been sinned against.

Conclusion

Could anyone successfully accuse us of eating with sinners? Eating with sinners is a call to be fearless in spite of hostility in engaging in God's service of extending a hand of friendship and fellowship to sinners. Eat with sinners, and fulfil the mission and mandate of God to rescue the perishing and care for the dying.

A Little Wine

THE 100TH ANNIVERSARY OF RED STRIPE BEER

> **Scripture Lessons: Isaiah 28:1-8; Proverbs 20:1-13; 1 Timothy 5:17-23**
>
> *"Drink no longer water, but use a little wine for thy stomach's sake and thine often infirmities" (1 Tim. 5:23 KJV).*

» 8 July 2018

The text says: "Stop drinking only water" (1 Tim. 5:23 NIV), but what is the context? Paul is not a doctor; he is giving folk wisdom advice. He is not saying do not drink water. He is saying drink water plus a little wine. It is for medicinal use. It is to aid digestion. This home remedy works.

Drinking a little wine is not binge drinking, which would be irresponsible; that would be greed and recklessness. Drinking a little wine is not encouraging drinking wine to "build a vibes" and feel sweet; it is not drinking to loosen the tongue and become boastful, "bumptious" and loose. It is not encouraging drinking wine to make a person more vulnerable to our charms and seduction, or for any other similar ulterior motive. It is not drinking wine to impair our judgment and decision making, making us utter strange things and entertain strange men. It is not for selfish pleasure.

Isaiah 28:7 says that a person is unwise who is overpowered by wine, wealth or women. A drunkard staggers and ridicules all that is serious and sacred. Here, wine is personified as doing what people do under its influence. The verse describes leaders raging, that is, being boisterous and noisy, no longer decent and lacking in restraint. Under the influence and overpowered by excessive use of wine, we are deceived.

The Bible uses the word wine to refer to both an alcoholic beverage and unfermented grape juice. Whether fermented or unfermented wine, it is meant for health purposes – like stomach ailments. The Bible is a practical book. It recognizes and affirms that the drinking of wine ought to be for health reasons. In other words, eating and drinking must be beneficial to the human body and overall well-being. Therefore, excessive eating or drinking should be avoided. Eat what is optimum for the human body to perform at its best in doing God's will. Drink wine to the amount that is optimum for the human body to perform at its best in doing God's work. Whatever we do, eat or drink, do it to the glory of God. "A little wine" means: as much as is necessary for maintaining health.

Paul was writing to Timothy as a father figure who is older and more experienced. Paul was considerate about Timothy's total well-being. Both Paul and Timothy had weak bodies, sicknesses, illnesses (Gal. 4:13-14). He warned against abstinence from wine when wine can help frail bodies. Paul's advice was to use all legitimate means to preserve health.

There are three considerations: avoid drinking wine for the sake of selfishness; have wine for the stomach's sake and drink wine for the soul's sake.

Avoid Drinking Wine for the Sake of Selfishness

The passage encourages a specific dosage of wine – "a little wine". However, due to greed, we take excessive amounts of wine, not realizing that it is a mocker. It is selfish to drink more wine than is necessary. It is self-centred to drink more wine than is needed. It leads to drunkenness. In such a state, people become garrulous, quarrelsome, cantankerous and deep down very unhappy.

People who are full of wine are pushing the envelope; testing the limit; showing off. Some engage in binge drinking, and some people living under the influence of excessive wine become godless. Such people scoff at God, feeling they know more than God, are smarter than God, and have no use for God. It is all about being intoxicated with one's self-importance and power. Drinking alcohol as a regular beverage means we are greedy and godless.

Excessive wine drinking promises pleasure it cannot deliver; excessive drinking and drunkenness cause pain. It mocks and exposes one to disgrace and scandal. When one is under the influence of strong drink, one scoffs at religion. It is the bad usage of wine that is prohibited. So, a deacon must not be given to wine (1 Tim. 3:3, 8). A deacon should never misuse wine.

Be sober and drink responsibly. Drink in moderation, so that we can be in charge of self, in charge of faculties, in charge of our reasoning and personality.

Have Wine for the Stomach's Sake

Before advanced medical research, Paul said that wine was good for the stomach and other ailments. Now it is confirmed that wine and grape juice provide us with antioxidants, which are good for the health of the heart, and in the fight against a host of diseases. The writers of the Bible, using folk wisdom, knew this, thousands of years before.

The drinking of a little wine must be done with the intention to improve our health, enhance healing and increase our wellness. There ought to be a purpose in drinking. It should be done to advance our prosperity. It should be done to facilitate us living well; it is about well-being.

Unfortunately, some people cannot get a sip of the wine. They are denied a little wine. All they get is coke, which inhibits and stunts their development. People who are working on road construction, not too far from here, cannot attend church because they have to work seven days a week. They cannot buy a little wine, because they are not paid the minimum wage agreed upon between the Incorporated Masterbuilders Association of Jamaica and the trade unions, and they are not paid overtime. How can we drink more than we need when others cannot get a little wine? Can a minimum wage earner really afford a little wine for the stomach's sake, or will they die for lack of a little wine for stomach and ailments?

Drink Wine for the Soul's Sake

By soul, I mean the total being. Who are we in essence and nature? We are both body and mind. Therefore, be Spirit-filled and Spirit-led.

Wine is now being used as a personification, a symbol and sign and representation, and re-presentation, of the blood of Christ. It is the wine representing the blood of Jesus. Therefore, do not despise the Lord's Table as if participating is optional. Just sip and see that the Lord is good, and experience pardon, pardon for the vilest of sinner. So instead of being drunk with wine, one can be filled with the Spirit, and be led by the Spirit to drink a little wine for holistic health.

Living in Praise of God – Celebration
THE 1989 JAMAICA BAPTIST UNION ASSEMBLY

Scripture: 1 Corinthians 10

» *23 February 1989*

Can one be holy and remain holy if one attends pagan celebrations or eats meat which has been part of a pagan celebration? That was the million-dollar question that the Corinthian church posed to Paul, expecting an answer. A decision was hard to arrive at because there were occasions when a believer would be invited to share in a feast or celebration which followed a pagan sacrifice, and it was accepted social practice to have meals in a temple or in some place associated with an idol. To have nothing to do with such events was to cut oneself off from most social interaction with one's friends, relatives and associates.

Paul knew that eating or not eating food cannot commend us to God. He further acknowledged that idols are just structures which are lifeless, powerless and useless: nonentities. However, offering food to these lifeless, powerless and useless idols in pagan temples was a dangerous business. This action was dangerous because of possible damage to the Christian faith of the weak brethren and, worse, it gave to an object the glory and honour that was rightly due to God. Eating meat in a pagan temple placed the people in the presence of demons. Nevertheless, sharing a personal meal with a pagan was different. To raise questions of conscience about the source of the meat at this meal of celebration was to be hypocritical rather than holy. It is hypocritical, because one would have to raise similar questions about the meat one ate in one's home, because any meat bought in a public market could probably have come from one of these pagan sacrifices. Such probing is pompous, because in accepting the invitation, one knew beforehand the likely source of the meat, so in such cases, the question was designed to embarrass rather than to enlighten. Such an inquiry was peripheral, because it ignored the more central need of eating to the praise of God with the intention of converting the pagan.

You see, our primary focus is really to praise God in eating, drinking or whatever we do. Paramount importance must be placed on celebrating the bounties of God, on recognizing that the earth is the Lord's and the fullness thereof.

The theme can be summed up in one word, "holiness", while the subject can be summed up in one word, "celebration". It is not much of an overstatement, perhaps not an overstatement at all, to say that the words "holiness" and "celebration" are synonymous. The two words are the two sides of the same coin, you cannot have one without the other. The reason for celebration is to celebrate holiness. Holiness leads to celebration. Celebrate in everything you do to the glory of God. Members of the Women's Federation, the Men's Brotherhood and the Christian Education Department, friends all, if we have been living holy lives, then we have plenty to celebrate and crow about. It is time to fling the gates open and praise. However, for us to appreciate, understand and engage in true celebration, we need to be aware of false celebrations.

FLEE PAGAN CELEBRATION

> *"...the people sat down to eat and drink and got up to indulge in pagan revelry"* (1 Cor. 10:7 NIV)

Pagan celebration is that type of celebration which is unholy. It is profane and sacrilegious. It gives honour that is due to GOD to someone else or something else. It is found where there is false worship or superstitious worship. It is a celebration that might have noise and laughter, but it is inspired by the devil.

Paul mentions examples of pagan revelry. To engage in sexual immorality is paganism (1 Cor. 10:8), because here sex is being used to celebrate an illicit relationship. It is pleasure without holiness. It is joy and ecstasy which God cannot be praised for. The January 1988 issue of the magazine *Caribbean Challenge* states that by age 18, 43 per cent of all teens in evangelical fundamentalist churches have had sexual intercourse. They made the startling observation that, in American society, the level of sexual promiscuity in the church is almost identical to that in the world. What of Jamaica and in particular the Baptist men, women and youths? This is virgin soil to be researched. However, could it be that the results would show that 90 per cent are sexually immoral while the other 10 per cent are liars? Sexual immorality should not be mentioned as happening among saints (Eph. 5:3), because it is pagan celebration. It is a cancer that can destroy fellowship. It breaks down the believers' resistance to other temptations and chokes the believers' attempts to live holy lives.

Even eating and drinking can be paganized. Eating and drinking without a concern for the physical needs and spiritual maturity of others make fellowship meals a pagan activity. Living to eat rather than eating to live can be the doorway to entering worse pagan celebrations (1 Cor. 10:7). All physical appetites must be controlled or else degenerate into pagan activities. Grumbling and griping are acts of paganism (1 Cor. 10:9-10). To worry about our needs is foreign to true saints. Matthew 6:32 states: "So do not worry, saying, 'What shall we eat?' or 'What shall we drink?' or 'What shall we wear?' For the pagans run after all these things..." (NIV). To murmur against God, to whine when we should worship, to sigh when we should sing, or to fail to trust God to supply our needs is to behave like a heathen rather than like a holy person.

Might I add that we must be careful of how we associate with any group, ideology, party or club that wants to rob the true and living God of the adoration that is His. Remember also that there are cults that are popular, powerful and widely promoted, but they are nevertheless pagan.

In our Christian education programme, we have to point out that many pop and dancehall songs are a cover for devil worship. They, in fact, create a desire for indulgence in immoral acts, including the use of drugs. The popular music scene can be a festivity of paganism.

Some of the political campaigning has degenerated into paganism and, if we are to believe one candidate, it has also degenerated into obeahism, which is an expression of paganism. The motorcades disregard traffic laws, massive meetings are held in places that cannot be properly policed, and the tenets of the Political Peace Accord have been openly and unashamedly broken by some candidates. Unfortunately, God is not placed first.

Paganism is not only outside the church, but it is also inside the church. It is not only at the doorstep of some churches, but it is the doorpost. Some Christian rites have been paganized. Marriage ceremonies have been trivialized, because participants are inadequately prepared for such a noble step, and the celebrants do not mean the vows they pledge. Sometimes the dedication of an infant is a farce, being little more than a social habit. Some of our rites, as implemented, have been paganized.

In fact, some churches could be so organized that their worship is one grand pagan celebration. If the Women's Federation is pulling one way and the Brotherhood another way, then this could be evidence of paganism. If the pastor, deacon or leader have in truth and in fact taken the place of God, then the church is pagan. The word of God in Isaiah 1:10-15 could be directed at our churches because of pagan practices.

"Stop bringing meaningless offerings! Your incense is detestable to me. New Moons, Sabbaths and convocations – I cannot bear your worthless assemblies. Your New Moon feasts and your appointed festivals I hate with all my being. They have become a burden to me; I am weary of bearing them" (Isaiah 1:13-14 NIV).

Are we guilty of condoning or participating in any of these pagan activities? Pagan celebration is false celebration, and we should flee it.

SURPASS PHARISAIC CELEBRATION

"If an unbeliever invites you to a meal and you want to go, eat whatever is put before you without raising questions of conscience" (1 Cor. 10:27 NIV).

Pharisaic celebration has a form of holiness, but not God's holiness. It is "wash over" holiness. This holiness has difficulty in maintaining

LIVING IN PRAISE OF GOD – CELEBRATION

the tension of true holiness. Therefore, the celebration of that type of holiness is usually dull.

What are the features of this type of celebration? Pharisaic celebration emphasizes the peripheral things rather than the integral issues; the minor over the major; and mistakes the circumference for the centre. It is more interested in raising irrelevant questions rather than celebrating, and questioning for questioning sake. Sometimes after two hours of an auxiliary meeting nothing has been accomplished. It is like supporting the trade embargo on South Africa and insisting that it means that one has to find out if the gold in one's ring comes from South Africa. Don't ask such questions; just wear the ring. However, if you know beforehand that the gold ring came from South Africa and you support the boycott, then don't wear ring.

Pharisaic celebration is a type of celebration that is pompous. This is when acts of celebration are done for the PR effect, when a great display of piety is done at the right time (usually Sundays) when most persons can see it. It is a willingness to engage in public prayers, which is not matched by practice of private prayers, a craving to lead but no real desire to follow our leader Jesus Christ. It is an overzealousness to preach, but no interest in spiritual discipline. Every good deed is discreetly or indiscreetly made known to all. Actions are used to draw attention to self rather than pointing towards God.

Pharisaic celebration is "privatized" celebration, that is "me, myself and I". Those people would see no need for church or assembly, no need to identify with, support or participate in auxiliaries.

Pharisaic celebration is privatized, pompous and peripheral and we must surpass it.

PURE CELEBRATION

> *"So whether you eat or drink or whatever you do, do it all for the glory of God" (1 Cor. 10:31 NIV)*

All we do must be to God's glory. In everything, give thanks. We must celebrate in all things. We must be holy under all circumstances. This is the real, genuine, unadulterated celebration of holiness. It is a celebration that thanks God for his gift of holiness. It is a celebration that praises God for maintaining us in a state of holiness. Pure celebration is holy celebration.

What if you don't feel like celebrating or you don't feel holy? Perhaps Hurricane Gilbert has devastated you, or poverty is creating

THREE ○ SPECIAL OCCASION SERMONS

havoc in your life. Your life has been marked by weakness and wickedness. You are hooked on pagan celebration and addicted to Pharisaic celebration. Not even going to church or singing a lively chorus helps. This state I believe is due to the fact that you are not recalling and appropriating what God in Christ has done for you, or you are not engaging in activities that nurture holiness. Putting it positively, you need to recall and appropriate what God in Christ has done for you and engage in activities that nurture holiness. Then you will want to celebrate.

Love must inform all conduct. Celebration must be infused by love: love for all, concern for all and being mindful of all.

For celebration to be obvious, then it is good for the brethren to dwell in unity – unity within groups and between groups; unity of purpose and goals. Accord on essentials is necessary.

Obedience to the word of God is a key pillar of celebration. It is the engine of celebration; it is the force behind holiness. On one occasion a woman in the crowd shouted to Jesus, "Blessed is the womb that bore you..." Jesus responded, "Blessed rather are those who hear the word of God and keep it!" (Luke 11:27, 28 ESV). It is greater joy and happiness to live in obedience to the word of God than to be the mother of the Messiah.

To trust God is to be "careful for nothing" (Phil. 4:6 KJV). Having a carefree indifference to things releases you to give your total energies to celebration. Having as your motto " seek first the kingdom of God" (Matt. 6:33 NKJV) gives you freedom to focus solely on celebration. When you are content in whatever state you find yourself, it means that you will always be praising, rejoicing and celebrating.

Yes, love, unity, obedience and trust are the four pillars on which holiness is built and this must inform and inspire celebration.

The passage points to some celebrative events. The Lord's Supper is a time of great celebration. It affirms the unity of all Christians and anticipates the oneness in Christ. It dramatizes God's love for us and our love for God and for each other. In the Lord's Supper, we are sharing in the benefits (justification and atonement) secured by the blood of Christ. To participate in the Eucharist is to share in the company of a people who, through union with Christ, has entered upon the new age. Therefore, the Lord's Supper should not be taken lightly. It should not be seen as that item called "any other business" on the agenda of the main worship service, or as a part of the service that can be missed. It is an integral part of the worship experience.

LIVING IN PRAISE OF GOD – CELEBRATION

That is why I am so glad to see that, on Sunday morning coming, at the largest congregation of Baptists in Jamaica, the Lord's Supper will be celebrated. Yes, the great event will be celebrated. Because of the importance of the Lord's Supper, we need to devise ways for participation in the Lord's Supper for those who of necessity have to miss the event on Sundays, and agitate for those who are forced by employers' actions to miss the Lord's Supper due to a seven-day work week. We need to address this matter to the Jamaica Employers' Federation, the trade unions and our parliamentary representatives, and if even the trade unions are lacking, then the Baptist Union must be found leading this matter. With a firm and strong voice, we must tell "the Pharaohs", "Let God's people go to celebrate the feast" (see Exod. 8:1). Yes, it is time to celebrate.

Sex in the context of marriage is a celebrative event. Too many men see it in terms of a conquest of the woman, and too many women see it as an opportunity to display their cunning over men. In fact, it is a gift of God to be engaged in with thanksgiving to God. Sex in that context of holy matrimony displays great love and the highest unity between two persons. It also gives a foretaste of heaven. Let us preach, teach, discuss and practise sex as a true celebrative event.

A time of eating and drinking is a time to celebrate the goodness of God's provisions. It is a time to praise God for all His good and perfect gifts. Let the Women's Federation, the Men's Brotherhood and the Christian Education Department, in your various social gatherings, be given to eating and drinking to the glory of God. Let family mealtimes be times of celebration of God's bounty. Let us eat with thanksgiving in our hearts. Harvests and harvest suppers should be great celebratory events where we leap for joy for the tender mercies of God towards us. We need to see God as our great benefactor and rejoice.

To proclaim the good news is to celebrate. One of the purposes of celebration is to witness "so that they may be saved", as Paul states in verse 31 (1 Cor. 10:31 NIV). The Women's Federation's motto encourages members to "seek, save, serve". To be involved in the process of salvation is our calling and our cause to celebrate. If we have something to celebrate, then we must have something to communicate. If we have something to shout about, then it means we have a story to tell. Celebration is a witness in itself, quietly heralding the good news. Celebration must lead to evangelism, and when the fruits of evangelism are seen, then it is time for more celebration. In heaven, there is joy over one sinner that repents, and on earth there should be great rejoicing when the prodigal returns. Let our baptisms take on a "carnival" atmosphere. Yes, when you witness any growth in the church, rejoice. Let the reception of new members into the church and its auxiliaries be a time of merrymaking.

Being a Christian is enough cause for celebration. The birth, ministry, death and resurrection of Jesus mean that we have entered into, and are living in, a celebration dispensation. Christ was ushered into the world on the phrase "I bring you good news of great joy" (Luke 2:10 AMP), and he began His public ministry by proclaiming the year of Jubilee, a celebration of the gracious provision of God (Luke 4:18-19). The Marys left the sepulchre with great joy because Christ is alive (Matt. 28:8). Yes, friends, it is celebration time. It is "bruckins" time. It is a time to have a Jesus Jam.

This celebration is just a warmup for the greater celebration. We are a pilgrim people on a motorcade to a greater celebration. It is going to be one "heaven of a party". We will be given to singing and dancing. We will learn a new dance called "sanctified steps". Then the elders will ask, "Who are these arrayed in white robes?" (Rev. 7:14 NKJV). These are they who have come through great tribulation, who have washed their robes in the blood of the lamb. These are those who have been holy among a people of unclean lips, who have been holy within unholy structures, who have been holy in the face of paganism and pharisaic celebration, who have been living liberated and revolutionary lives. It will be an all-night, all-day praise session. What an Amen that will be. What a Praise to the Lord it will be. What a Hallelujah that will be.

Conclusion

- Pagan celebration – flee it or repent of it.
- Surpass Pharisaic celebration because, though it has a form of holiness, it is not God's holiness.
- Engage in pure celebration, because it is celebrating holiness.

FOUR: HOME-GOING HOMILIES

FUNERAL FOR MAUD DALEY

> **Scripture Lesson: Psalm 23**
> *"The Lord is my Shepherd"*

» *31 July 2020*

The text "The Lord is my Shepherd" sums up the entire Psalm 23. "The Lord is my Shepherd is an introduction to the entire book of Psalms and, indeed, the text "The Lord is my Shepherd" is a brief account of the main points of the entire Bible. All that follows "The Lord is my Shepherd" in Psalm 23 is an expansion, explanation, exegesis and exposition of Psalm 23. In other words, because the Lord is my Shepherd, "I lack nothing" Ps. 23:1 (NIV). Because the Lord is my Shepherd, "I will fear no one" (PS. 23:4). Because the Lord is my Shepherd, he "anoints my head with oil" (Ps 23:5 NIV).

And who is this Shepherd? Jesus identifies himself with Psalm 23 when he stated, "I am the good shepherd" (John 10:11 NIV). Jesus feeds His sheep, Jesus protects His sheep, Jesus anoints the head of His sheep and, in fact, Jesus gave His life for His sheep. Therefore, in Jesus the Shepherd we can say: "I lack nothing" and "I fear no one" and "I am no nihilist".

FOUR • HOME-GOING HOMILIES

LACKING NOTHING

Psalm 23:1

Maudie knew the Psalms very well, and the Psalms describe her life and her relationship with God. She experienced the mercies of God, which were unmerited, undeserved and unearned. God's tender mercies towards her were more than enough, and so she lacked nothing. Maudie's testimonies, Maudie's life-story and Maudie's salvation history all declare: "I lacked nothing." So, for her, life was pleasurable, meaningful and hopeful. Maudie was satisfied, contented and fulfilled. It was not that she lacked ambition and drive. It was that she was satisfied with who she was and what she had accomplished, whether as a teacher, banker, wife, mother, deacon or administrator. When she worked in the bank, she told me not to envy a person you see driving a BMW, because she knew that some who were driving BMWs owed the bank a lot of money. Envy no one.

Do not be like persons who are not satisfied; not contented. They are restless. They are greedy. They want more than is necessary. Mary Trump, psychologist and niece of US president Donald Trump has published a book entitled *Too Much and Never Enough*. Some people are never satisfied, always complaining, always comparing self with others who have more possessions. That is sad.

Instead, we need to be contented with whatever state (Phil. 4) we find ourselves. Be contented, whether in plenty or poverty, imprisoned or free, in sickness or health. God is our provider, supplying our needs according to His riches in glory. Let this be our mantra: "I lack nothing." God gives us all the benefits of a child of God. Realize the privileges God offers. We will never ask God for a fish and he gives us a scorpion. Count the blessings one by one, and then you will realize that you lack nothing. God has supplied all we need to live a godly life. We lack nothing.

Do not worry, for God will make a way, was the saying of Deacon Maud as treasurer and finance chair of this church when we did not see the finances to take care of the expenses associated with the projects. Yes, God's hand was not short, He came through on time so we say: "I lack nothing." Believe God and say: "I lack nothing."

Funeral for Maud Daley

Fearing No One

"... though I walk through the valley of the shadow of death, I will fear no evil..." (Ps. 23:4 KJV)

The psalmist was fully aware that there were dangers, deadly perils and horrors on all sides, hence the need to rely on the power of the Shepherd with his staff and rod to protect. Having experienced such protection, the sheep fears no one. The call to fear no evil is not a pie in the sky statement by David. David was pursued by the powerful King Saul who wanted him dead but he said, "I will fear no evil."

But how can one be fearless in these difficult times when sister killing sister in Trelawny? How can we be fearless when there is the COVID-19 disease being imported? People are scared, frightened and nervous over the threat of death and diseases. We are going through dismal times of unemployment, underemployment and a devaluing Jamaican dollar.

The Lord is my Shepherd means that God is present in times of doubt, disease, devaluation and even death. God is tender and sensitive towards His sheep. God gives hope in the midst of change, crisis, chaos and confusion in life. God is always available when we feel helpless, hapless and hopeless. Therefore, move from fear to exercise faith in God, which is a wholehearted commitment to God and His will and His Word. God's presence and power is our strength and comfort. God also has our back as he protects us. Therefore, do not give in to your fears, but have courage and face the Evil One, evildoers, evil spirits and the evil system. Then, we can say, "I fear no one."

Additionally, David had to speak truth to power: that is, King Saul. Paradoxically, the tables turned and the prophet Nathan had to speak truth to King David when David became king and lost his way. Nowadays, people are afraid to speak the truth, the whole truth and nothing but the truth. The most they will do is whisper on their verandahs. There are times we will have to speak the plain, hurtful truth and cause "good trouble". Do not compromise when it comes to giving the factual account. Maudie was given to speaking the uncompromising truth. She was never afraid to give her opinion in meetings, even if unpopular. My association with Maud began in 1990, when she was a member of the Boulevard Baptist search committee that met me at the Pelican Grill in Montego Bay to encourage me to become the pastor of Boulevard Baptist Church. She was the only member of the search committee who told me that I did not have to stay at the

FOUR • HOME-GOING HOMILIES

Manse at 15 King's Drive. She did not think the duplex was appropriate for us, a family of five. Maudie feared no one. Let this be part of our legacy that we "fear no one".

In addition, Maudie did not fear the greatest enemy, death. The family said that she had stopped taking the medication. Maudie was ready to die and be with her Shepherd and Saviour. Let us be like Maudie and fear not even death. Let us live life in such a way that we can say, "I fear no one, and I lack nothing."

NOT A NIHILIST

"You anoint my head with oil." (Ps. 23:5 NIV)

All the biblical commentaries that I consulted stated that the anointing of the head with oil in this passage was the anointing that takes place on festive occasions such as a banquets; hence, this is also the context where the cup overflows. It was an overflow of blessings and prosperity. Perhaps this would have happened at the feast put on by Herod where the leading men of Galilee were in attendance or at the banquet of King Belshazzar where 1,000 noble men were present. After the anointing of the head, the food and drink were in abundance. That interpretation would fit well with the first point "I lack nothing" because of the abundant provisions. In addition, this interpretation of "thou anointest my head with oil, my cup runneth over" (Ps. 23:5 KJV) would be an explanation, expansion and exposition of the first verse "The Lord is my shepherd, I lack nothing" (Ps. 23:1 NIV).

Nevertheless, there is virtue in seeing the anointing as that which takes place at the coronation of a king: a magnificent celebration which was also a festive occasion. Furthermore, David was anointed as king. The anointing of the head with oil has political connotations. In addition, it would be remiss of me on the eve of Emancipation Day holiday not to mention the importance of political struggle for freedom and justice.

Furthermore, Maud told me that in her earlier days she was a political activist. And Christians ought to be involved in politics, and be interested in how the resources of God are handled, and whether persons who are poor have access to opportunities and resources. We must be involved in the affairs of the country. Maudie was a political activist, but not a nihilist. She was no anarchist. She was not a rebel without a cause. She was not anti-authority, anti-establishment, anti-good order or anti-just-and-fair rulers. She did not believe that all governmental authority was unnecessary and undesirable, nor that a society should be based on free association of individuals. Rather, Deacon Maud believed in equal rights and justice. She wanted to see the books balanced, and also that lives were balanced. She was in the line of other Baptist deacons such as Sam Sharpe, and Paul Bogle who struggled for the betterment of the people. Jamaica is crying out for political leaders who are not scrapping for themselves and their connections, but politicians who are fair, just, and of impeccable integrity.

Once you are a Christian, you are anointed to serve God's people and to ensure that God's people who are naked are clothed, who are hungry are fed, and who are imprisoned are visited. We were anointed to serve God's people sacrificially without counting the cost. Get involved in the political process and ensure that all God's children are treated justly.

Then we will hear from God: "Well done, thou good and faithful servant: enter thou into the joy of thy Lord" (Matt. 25:21 KJV). Enter and commune and dine with your Shepherd and Saviour.

Conclusion

Deacon Maud Daley knew God as her Shepherd – her provider, protector and political leader. Therefore, she lacked nothing, she feared no one, and she was not a nihilist. Let us make God our Shepherd, and let us testify: "I lack nothing"; "I fear no one"; and "I am not a nihilist". Let us commit afresh to trust God and fight for the betterment of God's people, so that we can hear, "Well done, thou good and faithful servant; enter thou into the joy of the Lord" (Matt. 25:21 KJV).

FOUR ● HOME-GOING HOMILIES

FUNERAL FOR DEACON DERYCK BROWN

Scripture Lesson: Song of Solomon 1:5
"I am brown and comely." (Adapted)

» *28 February 2020*

It is understandable that I looked to the Song of Solomon, because Deryck was married to Hyacinth (Cherie Crawford) from 1962, the same year Jamaica got independence, some 58 years ago. The Song of Solomon celebrates sexual love – Song of Songs 5 – but does not address the issues of law, covenant or the God of Israel. It is a romantic book about practical love life. The song is read on the Sabbath during the Passover, which commemorates the Exodus from Egypt.

Furthermore, it is reasonable to look to this text in Black History Month: "I am black, ruddy, brown and comely". Deryck was comfortable in his skin. Furthermore, last week Evon reminded me that the nickname given to him and his brother Deryck was "Brown Sugar". Suzanne Francis Brown in *Generational Cycles: A Family of Browns Across a Century of Change* (2000) says that "both Deryck and Evon were senior managers in the National Sugar Company and in some quarters were tongue in cheek called 'Brown sugar'" (p.12). Somehow, the nickname "Brown sugar" with the aroma of sweetness led to "I am Brown and comely".

I know that reasonable people can argue that in this text, "I am Brown and comely", the speaker was female. But then, in Christ, there is neither male nor female. We live at a time when we can choose our gender. But more importantly, in the Christian faith, the Song of Solomon is used as an allegory of Christ and his bride, the Church. Deryck was definitely a part of the Church, the body of Christ.

Brown sugar is comely. It is attractive and sweet. What are some of the other properties of brown sugar? It is soluble, and brown sugar crystals have a shine.

FUNERAL FOR DEACON DERYCK BROWN

Deryck's Christian heritage was important to his life, work and witness. Deryck's grandfather William Daniel Brown was a Baptist clergyman born in 1860, and he served as president of the JBU in 1909. His uncle was Baptist minister Balmain Clifford Brown. Deryck Brown's sweetness and winsome personality cannot be understood outside of his life-transforming encounter with God as revealed in Jesus the Christ and empowered by the Holy Spirit. Deryck Brown's performance and professionalism can only be properly understood through the lens of his dramatically life-altering experience of God. What sustained Deryck were his roots in the church. There are three properties of brown sugar that are comely and applicable to Deryck Brown, and they can offer a path to a meaningful and productive life, namely sweetness, shine and solubility.

JUST BE SWEET

Brown sugar sweet. Perhaps the best known and best loved quality of brown sugar is its sweetness.

As you heard from the many tributes, Deryck Brown was a sweet soul. He was a darling. He had a winsome personality. He was never into any "cass-cass". He was respectful. Perhaps because his grandfather and uncle were Baptist ministers, he was very sweet towards his pastor. He never looked down on others, but tried to elevate even those who were difficult to deal with.

Unfortunately, too many persons feel it is alright to be crass, boorish and rude. They are easily angered and often lose their tempers. They are proud to be miserable, angry and cross. Crudeness, callousness and coarseness are seen as manly virtues. It is seen by people making fun of a soldier who got "bun". It is seen by people recording a man on fire at a gas station and posting those pictures rather than helping the man to reach the hospital as quickly as possible.

What we need is more sweetness, a kinder, gentler society. Politeness is a gift from each person to the other expressed in the way we treat each other. Being courteous is showing or giving respect and honour to each other.

Being gracious is not a matter of convenience, but graciousness is something due to everyone without exception. Authentic good manners make a statement about the kind of human beings we are.

In the words of the national anthem, we ask God to "teach us true respect for all". Let us outdo one another in showing respect to all. Be courteous; be polite in remarks and actions; disagree without being disagreeable and disrespectful; if at all possible, seek win/win situations; and let our natural response be to seek common ground based on common humanity. Respect due.

JUST SHINE

Brown sugar crystals can shine; they have glossy surfaces. Deryck was a shining light. He was a performer. He did many good works without fanfare. Deryck was deeply involved at Boulevard Baptist Church in property development; financial management; church administration; Christian education; policy, protocol and procedures development and writing; constitutional reform; spiritual and practical care; staff welfare and more. He served effectively as chairman of finance, chairman of the diaconate and member of the property committee.

It was his idea for us to have a conference room; it was his idea for a songbook; it was his idea for an Elderly Health Fund; it was his idea for a wheelchair lift; it was his idea to write proposals on behaviour in meetings, and for resolving conflicts.

Deryck Brown was a wise man and we could depend on his counsel. He taught me where to sit in a meeting. Deryck had an impact on this church. He was a deacon in the mould of the late Eric Downie. Downie and Deryck cannot be replaced. There can be no replicas. They are once-in-a-generation personalities. They are like George Headley, Vivian Richards and Brian Lara – batsmen who are a cut above the rest and a rare breed. Deryck shone for 84 years. It was his time to shine and shine he did. Now it is our time to shine.

DO GOOD DEEDS

We too are called upon to have an impact and influence on church and society. Christians ought to be a pervasive and persuasive influence on a sinful society. We ought to make a significant difference in the lives of others. We must help meet the needs of those who lack. Let us have open hands, open hearts and open homes for persons who are genuinely needy.

What Jesus taught, he practised. In Matthew 9:36 we read: "When [Jesus] saw the crowds, he had compassion on them, because they were harassed and helpless, like sheep without a shepherd" (NIV). Jesus felt compassion for people in need. Do good, especially for persons who are vulnerable, such as individuals with disabilities, behavioural disorders and learning challenges.

There are responsible Jamaicans wondering aloud whether they have made a difference in this life. Did we make Jamaica a better place than it was when we arrived? What have we done that has had a lasting effect? Are we fearful about the future of our children and grandchildren? Was it worth the sacrifice of putting serving God above selfish interests, achievements and attainment? Deryck showed it was worth it, and we too should do good deeds. "Let your light shine before others, that they may see your good deeds and glorify your Father…" (Matt. 5:16 NIV).

BE SOLUBLE

What are some properties of brown sugar? It is sweet and the crystals shine, and we ought to shine by doing good deeds. We must have a sweet personality, and show respect to all in our conversations and attitude. There is one more property of brown sugar. Brown sugar dissolves in water.

The text is about a bride who melts in the arms of true love. One cannot appreciate Deryck without Hyacinth – a marriage made in heaven. They were submitted to each other, and both submitted to God. They planned together. They prayed together. They played together. They travelled together. They enjoyed each other's company. They were soluble, and therefore the two became one.

What an example for those who are married. Let this be our desire: that wife and husband be in one accord. Recognize that your marriage is a covenant between the couple and God. Find marriage meaningful, because we say each for the other and both for God. Let there be mutual submission and mutual servanthood.

In addition, Deryck Brown immersed himself in the Holy Spirit. He was soluble in the Spirit. He allowed the Spirit to control his life. He was led by the Spirit. He walked by the Spirit. He talked in the Spirit. He was full of the Spirit.

Friends, be filled with the Spirit. Let God control our lives and our destiny. Let God's desires be our desires. Let God's thoughts be our thoughts. Let God's ways be our ways. Let our mantra be: "Yet not my will, but yours be done" (Luke 22:42 NIV).

Remember that the same apostle who declared himself "the least of the apostles" and that he does "not even deserve to be called an apostle, because [he] persecuted the church of God" (1 Cor. 15:9 NIV) also maintained that he was not a whit [iota, bit] behind the very chiefest apostle – "I do not think I am in the least inferior to those 'super-apostles'. I may indeed be untrained as a speaker, but I do have knowledge" (2 Cor. 11:5-6 NIV). Rely on God. Depend on God. We are not better than anyone, and no one is better than we are.

Then in the end, it can be said of Deryck and of us that we have fought a good fight; we have finished the race; we have kept the faith; and henceforth is laid up a crown of righteousness for us. Then Deryck and all God's faithful people will hear from God: "Well done, thou good and faithful servant… enter thou into the joy of thy Lord" (Matt. 25:21 KJV).

Conclusion

What is the conclusion of the matter? Let our lives display the properties of brown sugar; let us display some comely virtues and values. Be sweet – respect all. Just shine – leave a legacy of good deeds behind us. Finally, be soluble – dissolve our lives, our being, into God's Spirit and let Him lead and direct our paths.

Funeral for Revd Luther Gibbs
FOUNDING PASTOR BOULEVARD BAPTIST CHURCH

Scripture Lessons: Ecclesiastes 3:1-22, Revelation 21:1-8
"The victorious will inherit this."

» 6 July 2019

According to the wisest man, Solomon, life is not a bed of roses. At best, life is a mixed bag. There are the vagaries of life. Life has ups and downs; crying and laughter; times of peace and a time for war; success professionally, but disaster personally.

But life is not only to be described in relation to the vagaries, but also the vanity of life, not only as a mixed bag, but also as meaningless. And for the writer of Ecclesiastes, life was worrisome (1:8); life was miserable (1:13) and life was distressing – "so I hated life,

Funeral for Revd Luther Gibbs

Figure 6. Luther Gibbs, CD, MA, Founding Pastor, Boulevard Baptist

Photograph by Devon Dick taken at Luther Gibbs' home on the 50th anniversary of the founding of Boulevard Baptist (9 February 2019)

because the work that is done under the sun was grievous to me. All of it is meaningless, a chasing after the wind. I hated all things I toiled for under the sun, because I must leave them to the one who comes after me" (2:17-18 NIV). Solomon discovered that a life of wealth, women and wielding power was meaningless, useless and vain. Death, that great equalizer of all humans, was like a plague and a curse on all humankind, making mockery of life and brutally ending life. Ecclesiastes relates the mixed bag of life to the meaninglessness of life. Is this really what life is about?

However, when we get a vision of the new heaven and new earth, then life has renewed meaning: the vagaries of life are no longer the only reality, and the vanities of life are not the sum total of life. It is only through Jesus that we can make sense out of life. The Old Testament makes no sense without the New Testament. Life has new meaning through the resurrection of Jesus.

Acknowledge the Vagaries of Life

There are the vagaries of life. Life is a mixed bag of spills and thrills, hills and valleys. There is poverty and plenty; pain and pleasure; problems and possibilities; victory and defeat. Every joy seems to be preceded by pain. Every good seems to be first preceded by anguish. It seems as if it is one step forward and two steps backward. So, all the technological advances have the serious downsides of lack of privacy and the potential for public mischief.

There are also events in life that we expect, and we can explain, but then there are unexpected and unexplained events. There are predictable and unpredictable occurrences. Life is mixed and life will be a mixed bag. We enter the stages of life, and we have to exit the stages of life. We bloom today and we wither tomorrow.

Michael Schumacher was a great German Formula 1 racing driver with a record seven World Drivers' Championship titles – perhaps the greatest of all time. He came out of retirement and then had a skiing accident. Now, for the last three years this great athlete has been a vegetable. Life is a mixed bag.

In fact, in the vagaries of life, some people get more bad than good. Some persons never get that so-called lucky break or "buss". The A students in high school are employed by the C students. The talentless seem to prosper and the clueless rule. Life so often is not fair. The reality is that life for many involves more downs than ups; we have more reasons to cry than laugh. Everything we touch turns sour. Everything we try seems to fail. This is a peculiarity of life. No wonder "donkey seh di worl nuh level". Some get more than their fair share while others suffer. "Puss an dawg nuh ave di same luck." Sometimes it will feel as if Satan is throwing the kitchen sink at us, and the system is rigged against us. It is as if we are trying to go up the down escalator. Some women live in fear of rape and abuse, while others live in safety and security. Some live well off the hog, while others only get pig trotters to eat. This is the reality of life. Revd Luther Gibbs knew the vagaries of life, having had to take the good with the bad, and having had to allow the wheat to grow with the tares.

Unfortunately, too many Christians nowadays are living in self-denial. People want a guarantee for success. People are relying on blind faith, rather than on a faith based on an experience with God, the record of their salvation history, and the greatness of nature. Some Christians speak over their day to guarantee success. So, naturally, no one speaks over his or her life about sacrifice and suffering, or about a desire for a compassionate heart for persons who are "dirt" poor. Everybody wants to lie in green pastures, but never to walk through the valley of the shadow of death. This position is an attempt to deny that there are vagaries of life. Life will not be smooth sailing all the time. There will be turbulence and bumps on the journey of life. Life will always be a mixed bag.

Accept That There Are Vanities of Life

Life is not a mixed bag only, but life according to Solomon is also meaningless. It is the condition the rich man was facing that made him feel in spite of his wealth, leadership and youthfulness that something was missing in his life. In spite of being religious and keeping the commandments, life needed something more. Life was sorrowful, meaningless and worrisome. For us, too, there seems no useful purpose, no game plan, no goal in sight, no lasting value to our effort, our work and our pleasure.

Because of the vanity of life and the meaninglessness of life, people often have an obsession with their legacy in today's world. Because of that obsession with our legacy and the significance of our contribution, we make valiant attempts at preserving our names, memory and achievements. Therefore, we engage in a rewriting of history wherein we oversell our accomplishments and try to effect an elimination of our errors, weaknesses and mistakes. So, people have claimed achievements that they do not deserve, or fail to acknowledge the role others have played in their success story. Yes, all is vanity, meaningless, sorrowful and worrisome.

Is the life I am living the best life has to offer me? Have you ever known a person who gave the best years of their lives to a company or business, and then wondered whether it was worth it? What will be said about our lives at our funerals? Is life some meaningless series of events? That would be life at its ugliest.

Luther Gibbs saw that life was meaningless, sorrowful and worrisome outside of Christ, so he made a decision to follow Jesus and also a commitment to full-time pastoral ministry so he could point others to a meaningful, purposeful quality life. Luther was not concerned about his personal legacy. He never listed his achievements, but he liberally praised his partner Beryl, and he just wanted God to be glorified, and the saints to mature in the Christian faith.

Appropriate the Victorious Life

There are vagaries of life and vanities of life that cause stress, which can be sudden, strident and sustained, thereby leading to havoc in our lives. This is a fallen world. From sin entered the world, it has been a fallen world. The fallen world is seen in a society in which God's original intention is not desired or implemented. It is a world that has not only fallen short of God's perfection, but it is also hostile to righteousness. It is a world in which sin dominates, and where sin controls the undertakings of that society. In this fallen world, fallen angels, demons, and principalities and powers hold sway.

However, get a vison of what can be, what ought to be, and what will be under God. Without that vision, we will perish. We become overwhelmed by the vagaries of life and stressed out by the vanities of life. However, a vision of a new heaven and a new earth gives new meaning and hope of victory. This new heaven and new earth are for a renewed people, in order for them to experience victory. This victory is a gift from God. Victory is assured. Make sure we are part of the victory parade. This victorious life is what Christians were given when we offered our lives to God. There are three features I would like us to focus on concerning this vision of a victorious life.

Funeral for Revd Luther Gibbs

This Victorious Life is a People-Dictated Life

A people-dictated life is a life in which people come first, even before procedures or policies. It is a people-centred ministry. This people-centred ministry is not an attempt at making the voice of the people the same as the voice of God, wherein the majority may dominate to the exclusion of people with minority opinion. A people-centred ministry does not play to the gallery to be popular with people. It is not seeking the applause of people. However, it is an acknowledgement that people matter. It is to put people first. It is to make people the centre of God's ministry.

Luther Gibbs was not liked because he was tall, dark and handsome, but because he was a lover of people and people loved him back. His mantra was: "If I can help somebody as I travel along, then my living shall not be in vain." He was a people person.

To experience victory over the vagaries of life, and to experience victory over the vanities of life, we ought to engage in a people-centred ministry. People were at the centre of Jesus' ministry; hence he spoke to the outcast woman at the well; this is also why he had time for children and placed them at centre of ministry, and why he healed on the Sabbath day. Get that vision and experience the victory in a people-centred life, and in a people-centred ministry.

A Victorious Life is a Purpose-Driven Life

A purpose-driven life in God is a victorious life. It is a life that is given to strengthen the saints and glorify God. We will know the will of God and walk in it. We will work for the Lord. We will keep and protect the Christian faith. We will worship God.

Finally, it is a paradise-directed life. It is a recognition that this life is not all to life, otherwise we would be men most miserable, sorrowful and tormented. There is a paradise of milk and honey. Honey is a symbol of that which cannot spoil or become stale. Milk is a symbol of nourishment. We get a foretaste now. God will work out everything in the end for "those who love God and are called according to his purpose..." (Rom. 8:28 NLT). This paradise-directed life means that, ultimately, good will triumph over evil, truth over falsehood, faith over fear, love over hate, and life over death through the power of the resurrection of Jesus.

FOUR ● HOME-GOING HOMILIES

FUNERAL FOR OLDEST WOMAN IN THE WORLD, VIOLET MOSSE-BROWN

> **Scripture Lesson: 2 Corinthians 1:1-4**
> *"Praise be to the God and Father of our Lord Jesus Christ, the Father of compassion and the God of all comfort, who comforts us in all our troubles, so that we can comfort those in any trouble with the comfort we ourselves receive from God." (2 Cor. 1:3-4 NIV)*

» *7 October 2017*

The Father's gift of comfort for us in Jesus is for all persons, without exclusion or exception. God the Father's gift of comfort for us in Jesus is for all at no charge to us. All comforts come from God to us. God comforts us above all expectations. God thinks of every conceivable comfort for us. God the Father would not spare his only Son, so that we would be comforted. Jesus died and was raised from the dead, so that we may enter into everlasting comforts. God will comfort us to such an extent that no request for comfort will be left unanswered. The eye has not seen, nor the ear heard what comforts the Lord has in store for us. When God is comforting us, there is no stone left unturned in order to comfort us. God provides the comforts of green pastures, still waters, paths of righteousness, a prepared table and an overflowing cup. In addition, "thy rod and thy staff they comfort me" (Ps. 23:4 KJV). This is a God of abundant comforts.

Old age is an honour. And we honour people who are elderly by seeing to their comfort. The way society treats and offers comfort to the elderly is an indication of how Christian we are. Be a comforting family and community. This type of comfort is what people who are sick, old and dying need and deserve.

Funeral for Violet Mosse-Brown

Afflict the Comfortable

There are those who are comfortable in Zion. These people prey on old ladies. They take advantage of the elderly. They are worse than scavengers, because they will not even wait until the person has died before they seek to profit. Those people need to be confronted and condemned.

Corinth was a sinful city. There was easily available and accessible prostitution for the sailors. And even in the church, some Christians were boasting about a young man being intimate with his father's wife, and some Christians were getting drunk at the Lord's Table. These people who were comfortable in sin had to be confronted by St Paul.

We have similar problems in Jamaica. Underage girls, perhaps for economic reasons, are auctioning their bodies for money. Some underage girls are used as escorts to do the bidding of these dirty, rich old men. We need to deal with these men ruthlessly and quickly. The answer is not to beat one's daughter with a machete, but rather to beat these men with the long arm of the law. There must be harsh punishment and long rehabilitation behind bars for these filthy men.

Comfort the Afflicted

We ought to comfort those who are afflicted. Sometimes we make older persons feel unwanted, unappreciated and like a liability. We know that racism – prejudice, discrimination and antagonism against someone of another race based on the belief that one's race is superior – is wrong. We know that sexism – prejudice, discrimination and antagonism against women based on the belief that a man is superior – is wrong. But we fail to recognize that ageism – prejudice, discrimination and antagonism on the grounds of age based on the belief that youth is superior – is also wrong. We must support and comfort the elderly.

This comfort is not pity. Comforting a person is not telling them not to cry. Jesus was moved with compassion when the people were hungry after days in the desert. Jesus was moved with compassion when he saw the people suffering from diseases and poor health care, "Jesus had compassion on [the two blind men] and touched their eyes. Immediately, they received their sight and followed him" (Matt. 20:34 NIV). Jesus was moved with compassion when the people were desirous of teaching and the truth: "When Jesus landed and saw a

FOUR ● HOME-GOING HOMILIES

large crowd, he had compassion on them, because they were like sheep without a shepherd. So, he began teaching them many things" (Mark 6:34 NIV). Jesus was moved with compassion when they were distressed, depressed and dismayed: "When [Jesus] saw the crowds, he had compassion on them, because they were harassed and helpless..." (Matt. 9:36 NIV). The writer to the Hebrews said Jesus understands our weaknesses, fears, desires and hopes. Jesus is interested in human affairs and human needs, especially the basic and fundamental needs. Jesus' ministry was one for the body and the soul. It was holistic. He forgave sins and he healed bodies. He comforted the afflicted when they were crying. He gave hope to people who were harassed, hapless, hopeless and helpless. To comfort someone is to feel the suffering of others, and also to have the willingness to make a significant difference in the lives of others in need.

On Monday, Garth Rattray, family doctor and *Gleaner* columnist, said people are dying because of inadequate medical treatment. He gave two examples of persons in their 70s. Those people died. Perhaps they could have lived as long as Sister Brown. We all know persons like that who die of preventable diseases and due to the lack of adequate healthcare. Last month, an adherent of the Boulevard Baptist told me she had an appointment at a public hospital for next year and she needed treatment urgently! There are many ill and sick persons who need the comfort of proper healthcare.

Violet Mosse-Brown was not in the best of health when I visited her unexpectedly. After paying homage, I took my leave from her bedroom, and after some more pleasantries with other family members, I indicated my intention to take my leave. However, I was told that I could not leave because Sister Violet Mosse was leaving her bed to come to the verandah to bid me farewell. She went the extra mile in graciousness, in spite of age and infirmities. She was a celebrity, but she had class and an appreciative spirit. She was a warm-hearted person and a blessed soul. She made me feel comfortable. We need to perceive a need without anyone having to tell us or beg us or bargain with us or badger us. Be close to the people, so we can hear their cries and feel their pain. We ought to respond appropriately to the real, genuine, complex, acute, urgent needs of the people.

It would be remiss of me at the funeral for the oldest person in the world not to speak about long-term care (LTC). I will draw heavily on a study done by my daughter Dana-Marie Dick for her MSc in actuarial management for City University, London. LTC refers to a range of medical and social services that support the needs of people whose ability to perform everyday activities, such as toileting, dressing, eating and bathing has been diminished. The need for LTC could be the result of chronic illness, mental or physical disability, the ageing process, or serious injury from which the person is not expected to recover. Elderly persons are often neglected by family members. We are talking about 60 per cent of persons over the age of 65 who will require this LTC.

The government must step in and make special provision for LTC, including housing and supervision. The private sector, the providers of health insurance, and life insurance policies need to design specific products to help with long-term care.

Conclusion

Sister Brown, "well done, thou good and faithful servant… Enter thou into the [comfort] of thy Lord" (Matt. 25:21 KJV). Sis Brown did not get an official funeral, but she get a WD, a "well done", from God and will enter into the comfort of the bosom of Abraham.

Funeral for Aaron Jordan Miller, a Teenager

Scripture Lesson: Psalm 34
"The Lord is close to the brokenhearted" (Ps. 34:18 NIV)

» 10 September 2016

Why me? When tragedy occurs and we ask "why me?", it affirms that some bad things have happened to one, and not another. It therefore seems to confirm that life is not fair. At times, it resembles a game of chance with some getting the lucky breaks, and most getting heartbreak. And sadly, there are times when life is more like Russian roulette with its potential deadly consequences. Life is not fair with its inequalities, inequities and iniquities.

FOUR • HOME-GOING HOMILIES

When life throws up these harsh knocks, when the world is a hostile environment, when life is a rat race and the devil-take-the-hindmost, then we look to the God of the Psalms. Why? It is because the psalmist is a real person with issues like us, and who wears his emotions on his sleeve. When the psalmist was down and depressed, he said in the 22nd Psalm, "My God, my God, why hast thou forsaken me?" (KJV). The psalmist was pursued by a powerful king and felt abandoned by God in his hour of need, so much so that people were mocking him, asking, where is your God? (42). It is in these Psalms that we see the agony of suffering when the psalmist said "tears have been [his] food day and night" because of his enemies" (Ps. 42:3 NIV). No wonder he wanted sudden destruction to befall his enemies. However, it is the Psalms that offer insight into life, purpose in suffering and death, and hope in eternal life. So, we turn to our text in Psalm 34:18, for obvious reasons, where it reads: "The Lord is close to the brokenhearted" (NIV).

BRACE FOR HEARTBREAK

Life has heartbreak. Life has hard knocks. Life offers us setbacks to our well-ordered plans. Life has reversals that we cannot avoid, stop or escape from. Life throws up suffering and sorrows that overwhelm us. Our spirits are oppressed. The calamities are severe. It is a life not of "True Blue" (Jamaica College), but rather a life of "feeling blue".

Oftentimes the heartbreak comes upon us suddenly, unexpectedly and without warning. The heartbreak and the setbacks are like freak storms. Where did this come from? Remember Jesus in the boat with disciples who were experienced fishermen, and all of a sudden, a storm developed. Then, they started to blame Jesus, "how him a sleep" when "fire deh a muss-muss tail". Sometimes heartbreak does not follow any discernible trend. We just have to brace for heartbreak.

The death of Jordan was a serious heartbreak. It was not gentle and mild. It was terminal. Many persons said they did not know what to say to the family. My wife Mary was crying and saying she could not go to visit Debra, Rohan, Daniel and Joshua, Arielle because she did not know what to say. This one was hot, hurtful and cruel. However, we all need to brace for heartbreak.

You know, heartbreak is sure. They will happen to us sooner or later. They will happen in one form or another. The degree of the heartbreak differs from situation to situation, but all experience heartbreak. On

Funeral for Aaron Jordan Miller, a Teenager

Wednesday, a friend had to comfort a mother whose child committed suicide. That was a heartbreak if ever there was one. On Tuesday, Baptist member Orville Clarke was killed in front of his three children. Clarke was the brother of Baptist pastor Orlanzo Wright. In Clarendon, some three years ago, Clarke identified some persons who killed people in that parish, and afterwards sought refuge in another parish. However, his mother became ill, and so he went back to Clarendon to help his mother, but he did not realize that these criminals have long memories, and so his two-year-old, five-year-old and eight-year-old are fatherless. Life has heartbreak. It is inevitable. It happened to the psalmist, to Job, to Paul and to Jesus. And it will happen to us.

So, when we say, "Why me?" it could be selfish, because it could imply also that it should not happen to me, but to someone else. It is to feel self-righteous, and to claim that we have done so much good, so "Why me?" Sometimes in our twisted logic, we even feel that we have done something bad, so this is why it has happened to us. So, when these heartbreaks and hurts come, it is not a time to say, "Why me?"

One cannot experience setbacks and remain the same. We are different for life. We are changed for life. We can become bitter or better. We can engage in self-pity or regain our self-worth and self-esteem; we can become resentful or become renewed; we can become a person walking around with hurts or become happy. There is an Anglican priest, Julie Nicholson, who gave up the priesthood after her eldest child was killed in the London bombings on a train a decade ago. She said she could not forgive that bomber.

Heartbreak is a part of life. Pop culture sings about heartbreak. Canadian singer Justin Bieber's sad song "Love Yourself" is about heartbreak. Also, Barbadian singer Rihanna's "Love the Way You Lie (Part 2)" is a song about a heartbroken person. American singer Beyoncé sings a sad song in "Irreplaceable". Finally, there is the classic "Total Eclipse of the Heart" by Bonnie Tyler. These songs remind us that heartbreak is part of life.

Be Happy

Rohan's constant mantra was that his son Jordan's aim in life was to be happy. Jordan had big dreams of investing money and making money, not as an end in itself, but to buy the things he wanted. He wanted to be happy. He had his cave in the house, and he was creative. He wanted his space to be happy. He understood his schoolwork, not as an end in itself, but as a means to pursue happiness. He understood conversation as an opportunity for his father to listen to him, understand him and agree with him. That was happiness for him.

God wants human beings to be happy. Gen 1:28 speaks of God blessing Adam and Eve. This blessing meant they were empowered to pursue happiness. God wanted them to experience peace of mind, fulfilment and happiness.

The United States Declaration of Independence (1776) speaks about the right to life, liberty and the pursuit of happiness. All can agree that life is special and sacred. Most believe that we ought to be free and no one should enslave us. However, why does the pursuit of happiness get equal billing to life and liberty. Why is happiness a fundamental right in the US Declaration of Independence? This is because an important purpose of life is the attainment of joy for oneself, once we do not violate the rights of others or engage in illegal and immoral means to attain happiness. Live life in a way that makes us happy.

Is happiness to be found on Wall Street? Hell, no. Is it to be found in the 2006 movie *The Pursuit of Happyness* starring US comedian Will Smith? This rags-to-riches story has informed the focus on wealth accumulation for selfish purposes, personal safety and security as the only important issue in the pursuit of happiness. Subconsciously, we assume that happiness is about fame and fortune. Happiness is not about personal pleasure for me, myself and I, nor jokes at other people's expense. Happiness is not about being a diva, whether fluffy or curvy. It is not about an egoistic, hedonistic life. It is not about being ahead in the rat race. It is not about overindulgence. Rather, the pursuit of happiness is finding riches in rags. It is making lemonade when life sends lemons. It is turning a heartbreak into something beautiful.

Horatio Spafford (1828-88), successful US lawyer, real estate investor and Presbyterian elder, sent his wife and children ahead of him on a boat for a vacation. Catastrophe struck the boat and all four of his daughters died. After that calamity, he penned the words of a hymn with the title "It is Well with my Soul". It meant he was happy in his soul.

Happiness is about peace of mind. It is about finding joy in the simple things of life, such as nature walks, star gazing, family

Funeral for Aaron Jordan Miller, a Teenager

vacations, a few close friendships, limiting desires to what are truly necessary in life. Live a simple life. That is happiness.

How can we find happiness in this dark world of heartbreak? It starts with the Lord God being close to us. This closeness is due not to him drawing close to us, but rather us drawing close to him in our time of sorrow. It is LISTENING to God. It is being obedient to the word of God. God is ever near to us.

It is about God being in solidarity with us. It is about Jesus saving us not from disaster, but saving us in disaster, danger and death. We will not be immune to danger. There is no guarantee that we will never experience another heartbreak. However, what is sure is that God is with us during and after the heartbreak. Then and there begins the process of becoming happy again when God satisfies our longings. "Weeping may last through the night, but joy comes with the morning" (Ps. 30:5 NLT). Weeping is for a short time, like a guest who comes for lodging for an evening, but joy comes with the morning. Evening gives way to the morning. The morning will come without the sorrow. A day will come in the afterlife when there will be no more tears and sorrows.

God is in solidarity with us in our heartbreak. God is not absent in times of trouble. We mistakenly believe that God is absent when we are in the deepest hole. In the Gospel of John, chapter 11, both Martha and Mary on two different occasions said to Jesus, "… if you had been here, my brother would not have died" (John 11:21, 32 NIV). The thought is that death is the sign of the absence of Jesus – far from it. Time and time again, the psalmist made the point that "God is our refugee and strength, a very present help in trouble" (Ps. 46 KJV). God is present in our sorrows. God hears our cries. He understands our sighs. He will make us wiser, stronger and kinder. We will have a better understanding of God. We will have a better appreciation for life. We will cherish family even more.

Psalm 23 reminds us that "though I walk through the valley of the shadow of death, I will fear no evil: for thou art with me" (Ps. 23:4 KJV). The gospel of Matthew is about the presence of God from start to finish. Jesus was named Immanuel meaning "God with us" (Matt. 1:23): God in solidarity with us, and God identifying with our needs, fears and hurts. The Gospel of Matthew ends with "lo, I am with you always, even to the end of the age" (28:20 NKJV). God is in solidarity with us unto the end.

FOUR ● HOME-GOING HOMILIES

Death is our last enemy. Through Jesus' death, death was conquered. Just like a seed dies and comes back to life, so Jesus in dying conquered death. Through Jesus' resurrection, good triumphs over evil, happiness over heartbreak, and life over death.

Last night, at the prayer meeting, Mrs. Aldena Miller, Rohan's mother, requested this song which I close with: "God will take care of you", because the Lord isqcrvce2sw1aq close to heartbroken people.

FUNERAL FOR KAYLA RICHARDSON, A CHILD

Scripture Lesson: Job 9
"His wisdom is profound, His power is vast." (Job 9:4 NIV)

» *11 August 2008*

HOW COME?

Some people get an advantage in life based on the country in which they were born in, and what family name they have, and which school tie they wear. In addition, life turns up some hard knocks. A couple of weeks ago, a funeral service was held here for a woman, forty years old, who, after delivering her first child, developed complications and died a few days later. Additionally, maternal grandfather of Kayla, Morris Wynter, was telling me that, recently, a husband and wife were killed in an accident when a bus ran a red light near Weymouth Dr., and yes, three-year-old Kayla Richardson tragically died a few days ago. Life has its hard knocks. Life does deal us these unfair disadvantages.

But when life throws up these hard knocks, we need to listen to the innocent voices. Yes, listen to Kayla. Whenever Kayla was called to a gathering, she assumed that it was a call to devotions (worship of God). She associated gathering together as a call to attend devotions. This on the surface might appear to be a simplistic association with devotions at school. However, let us look deeper at what Kayla could be saying, or what God might be saying to us through

FUNERAL FOR KAYLA RICHARDSON, A CHILD

Kayla. As we all know, out of the mouth of babes and sucklings. God has ordained wisdom and strength. What lesson was God teaching us through Kayla? I believe it is this: that all our actions, our going out and coming in, ought to be seen as opportunities for worship. Remember that Matt 18:20 says, "For where two or three are gathered together in my name, there am I in the midst of them" (KJV).

All our actions ought to be ordained by God, and therefore our service ought to be acts of worship. Rom. 12:1 says, "Therefore, I urge you, brothers and sisters, in view of God's mercy, to offer your bodies as a living sacrifice, holy and pleasing to God – this is your true and proper worship" (NIV). Your bodies (life, persona, personality) ought to be used in the act of worship. That is God's word to us through Kayla. Unfortunately, even some Christians compartmentalize life. Worship is only what is done at church on a Sunday, but worship of God is excluded from partisan political party positions. In addition, when we bring God to the workplace, it is just the ten-minute devotion on the Monday morning, but it is not demonstrated through quality service to customers and truth telling to the clients. Additionally, worship does not affect our sex life: in fact, for some sick, perverted minds, it is appropriate to abuse children, even babies, sexually. Kayla is calling us, at this funeral service, to devotions, which is not confined only to this thanksgiving service, but should also be seen in how we conduct ourselves at the graveside, at the reception, and in what we say and how we comment to the parents. That too is worship of God. Let us worship God every time and in every way at home, at church, and in the community.

The second statement from an innocent child came from Kayla's brother Daniel. Within hours of the death of his only sister, he said that Jesus has the power to protect, and that Jesus has made a choice. The God who we ought to worship every day and in every way is the one who has the prerogative to make certain decisions. He decides what he will allow. He allows it to rain on the just and the unjust. He decides the times and seasons for the return of Christ. He establishes kingdoms and allows them to fall. Daniel's comment is a statement about the power of God. There are certain things we do not have any control over. We cannot prevent lightening. We cannot prevent hurricanes; all we can do is to prepare for them as best as we can. God is all powerful. No matter how powerful a person is, it is just for a time. Whether it is politics, sports, church or business, we are just here for a time. We play our part, and then we move on. Just place your hands in the hands of the man from Galilee.

Sometimes when it seems like evildoers prosper; when we see wicked people getting all the breaks; when we see Satan touching a family's heath, wealth, children and happiness, we sometimes wonder who is in charge. It is our God who reigns. He is all powerful. Nobody can frustrate the will of God. The battle between God and Satan has been won already by God. Christ on the cross has disarmed all principalities and powers. He has put to shame the forces of evil on the cross. And in Jesus we are more than conquerors.

The third child I would like to quote this afternoon is Kayla's father, Dalton. Some of you might dare to question my portrayal of Dalton as a child. Dalton cried like a baby for his daughter. Even his brother Michael was shocked, saying that he knew Dalton as a strong person not given to tears. Yes, that fateful night, he cried like a baby, and in that baby state he made some babblings. He asked, "Why me?" but not why me, meaning it should happen to someone else instead of him. He was not being selfish, but was rather feeling the pain of the situation. In fact, he was blaming himself. I had to remind him that he did the best he could. He tried to avoid the accident, and the driver of the vehicle who drove into him had already said he was sorry. Dalton was not selfish, because he asked why he did not die and save the innocent Kayla. He was concerned more about his daughter's welfare and well-being than his own. He thought more highly of Kayla's life than his own. Does it not remind you of Jesus who said he came not to be served but to serve? (Matt. 20:28). Doesn't it remind you of Jesus who said: "Greater love hath no man than this, that a man lay down his life for his friends"? (John 15:13 KJV). Jesus loves us and died on our behalf, so that we might have life, and life more abundant (John 10:10). What a better world this would be if we understood the implications of Jesus dying on our behalf out of love for us? What a different world, if we would love one another as Jesus loves us?

"God knows best," was the utterance of Kayla's mother, Kay. This demonstrates Kay's childlike faith in God. It reminds us of the verse that says, "Whoever does not receive the kingdom of God like a child will not enter it..." (Mark 10:15 NASB). It is a great belief that God knows best, and does best, and always acts in our best interest. For a mother to say that over and over again, just minutes after the death of her only daughter, is a demonstration of unshakeable faith in the grace, wisdom and love of God. As we go through the valley of the shadow of death, we fear no evil because he who is with us knows best. In addition, "all things work together for good to those who love God, to those who are called according to His purpose" (Rom. 8:28 NKJV). God can work out things. When God allows bad things to happen, it is not the absence of love, but a confidence in our ability to endure and overcome. Satan made the allegation that Job was only worshipping God because good things were happening for Job. Satan bet God that, if bad things happened, then Job would leave God. I can imagine Satan's allegation concerning the Richardsons. So many good things are happening for the family. Let us touch them with a death and see what will happen. However, God has confidence in you, that through it all you have learnt to trust in Jesus. As the saying goes, the strength of tea is not known until you put the tea bag in hot water. True character is displayed in how we react during tragedy. I remember Kay saying to my wife Mary at Andrews hospital, "Watch my mother." In her distress and her uncertainty, she had time to be concerned about her mother.

This accident and death are not memories that will go away. They are part of your family history. Your continued reaction will determine how strong your family will be. Dalton and Kay, you need to be strong for each other, and for your son Daniel, and he who knows best will take care of you.

Civilla Durfee Martin (1866-1948), Canadian American hymn writer, wrote:

> "Be not dismayed, whate'er betide, / God will take care of you! / Beneath his wings of love abide, / God will take care of you!" (1904)

You might have expected a better funeral sermon experience than to listen to the babbling about childlike faith. However, shades of their utterances can be seen in Job. Kayla's call to worship reminds you of Job's call to worship. After Job had lost children and property, he fell down and worshipped (Job 1:20). "The LORD gave, and the LORD has taken away; Blessed be the name of the LORD" (Job 1:21 NKJV). Daniel saying that it is Jesus' choice reminds us of Job 9:4. Job recognizes that he cannot argue with God: "His wisdom is profound, his power is vast" (NIV). Dalton's questions remind us of Job's question in chapter three which led in the end to his self-giving (Job 3:11). Kay's childlike faith reminds us of Job who refused, in spite of urging from his spouse, to curse God and die (Job 2:9-10). Job did not believe it made no sense to serve a God who allows Satan

FOUR ● Epilogue: Evangelistic Exhortations

to cause so much havoc – God knows best. But I believe that God spoke to us through Kayla – worship is full-time. He spoke through Daniel – Jesus makes a choice; it is his prerogative because he is all powerful. God spoke through Dalton – Jesus died on our behalf and we must be prepared to exhibit that quality love for our loved ones. God finally spoke through Kay – God knows best.

Epilogue:
Evangelistic Exhortations

REPENT AND BE BAPTIZED

> **Scripture Lesson: Acts 2:22-38**
> *"Peter replied, 'Repent and be baptized, every one of you, in the name of Jesus Christ for the forgiveness of your sins. And you will receive the gift of the Holy Spirit'."*
> *(Acts 2:38 NIV).*

» *3 May 2015*

We have in this verse the summary of Christian doctrine as regards human and God. Humans are called to repentance and faith in God, while God forgives humans of sins and offers us the gift of the Holy Spirit. And both of these are expressed in the sacrament of baptism, which as it were ties the act of humans to the promise of God, for the sacrament expresses humans' faith in God and repentance towards God, and also God's forgiveness and gift. This verse is saying that forgiveness of sin is only obtained in the name of Jesus, the same Jesus the Jews had before rejected, and whose identity as Messiah they denied. However, upon their repentance toward God and their profession of faith in our Lord Jesus, the Christ, they were to be baptized in his name and by his authority, according to his command, and living by faith in him. The apostle exhorted them to repent of their sins, and to **openly** declare their belief in Jesus as the Messiah.

There Needs to Be Remorseful Confession

There needs to be sorrow and remorseful guilt over what is happening in Jamaica. We need to be saddened by "what a gwaan". There was a five-year-old gyrating on video, and adults giving her money as enticement. In this very Child Month, many girls are being sexually abused and raped by relatives.

Jamaica has cable operators who have been broadcasting unauthorized content for years. We need remorseful confession. On Friday, more persons accused Bill Cosby, the famous actor, of sexual assault and rape. However, I wonder what we ourselves would do if some persons whom we hold in high esteem are scumbags? We need to express godly sorrow, because we have turned a blind eye to respectable people who engage in outlandish sin against women and God.

Remorse is shame that you feel because of your actions. To feel remorse is to regret your actions. Remorse is a sense of guilt over your actions, or inactions, and a desire to do the right thing. It is godly sorrow.

There is a website which claims that affairs help marriages. Ashley Madison exists to help married people have affairs. Even if true, it does not mean adultery is a good thing. God can make good out of bad. A mother might sell her body to pay school fees, and then her child does well at school and becomes a doctor, but it does not mean prostitution is good – but God can make good come out of bad. A woman might have a child out of wedlock with a married man, and the child becomes a lawyer; it does not mean the sin was okay, but that God can make good out of evil. So, we are left with expressing godly sorrow for all our sins.

What is Remorseful Confession?

A remorseful confession is an expression of sorrow or regret, and an acknowledgment of fault, a shortcoming or a failing. Nobody is perfect, and neither is any organization – we all make mistakes. Things can and will go wrong. In such circumstances, we should make a remorseful confession, such as an acknowledgement of the wrong done, or an assurance that a problem has been addressed or will not recur.

FOUR ● Epilogue: Evangelistic Exhortations

There Needs to Be Radical Change

A failure to acknowledge fault, and even partial apologies, will not lead to radical change. Some will say, "I'm sorry this happened," but that is not necessarily radical change. Radical change is to uproot everything. Repent – the word denotes a change of mind. It is like moving from darkness to light. It is a massive and distinctive change. It is like going one direction, and then doing an about-turn.

Why Is It Often Difficult for People to Repent?

It is a fact of life that most people do not like to admit they are wrong – which is a necessary precondition to a sincere repentance. Reasons why people often find it difficult to admit fault and to repent may include:

- Being wrong is a truth many people don't wish to face;
- Concern that repentance could be seen as a sign of weakness;
- Concern about confirming responsibility for something that was otherwise only speculated or assumed;
- A reluctance to acknowledge inappropriate behaviour: too often we fail to accept responsibility for our actions, or ownership of the problem.

To repent is change our minds and entertain other thoughts. A change of mind will produce a change of actions in life and conversation. Repent and make an open and heartfelt confession of your sin. Be convicted about sin and hate sin and forsake sin.

Proverbs 1:10 warns: "My son, if sinners entice thee, consent thou not" (KJV). This a solemn warning against temptation. Say, "I will not," and abide by it; be deaf to all their entreaties and all their persuasions. Flee the very appearance of sin (1 Thess. 5:22).

Resolute Commitment

We must be willing to express remorseful confession; there needs to be desire for a radical change, and we must have resolute commitment to this new life. It is a commitment to change from habitual sin to holiness. The conversion here spoken of is confined to a change in the present state of mind, moving to point one's life in a new direction. The apostles had displayed rivalry, jealousy, ambition, and they needed to turn away from such failings. They needed to learn a different lesson: become as little children. Christ points to little children as the model to which the members of his kingdom must align themselves. The special attributes of children which he would recommend are humility, simplicity, and being teachable. It is an intentional commitment to change. It is a sincere desire to follow Jesus.

Romans 12:2 says: "And be not conformed to this world: but be ye transformed by the renewing of your mind, that ye may prove what is that good, and acceptable, and perfect, will of God" (KJV). Have a spiritual transformation and new motives. Engage in spiritual exercises, reading and meditation on the scriptures, and prayer, and also participate in the Lord's Supper.

AFTERWORD

The construct of our times has created among many listeners of the word an insatiable appetite for "frilly" sermons that appease the conscience and leave us feeling good without any sense of responsibility or accountability. I am deeply honoured to be asked to contribute the Afterword to this publication by the Revd Dr Devon Dick, *Preaching in Jamaican Seasons*, a collection of biblically sound sermons preached at significant moments throughout the 35 years of his pastoral ministry.

My encounters with Revd Dr Dick had mostly been passing, until I served as aide to him during his presidency of the Jamaica Baptist Union, and encountered him behind the scenes as he prepared to preach each of the first three sermons published in this book. It was then that I met the preacher who was not simply adept at interpreting and proclaiming the word, but just as importantly one who embodied the word. As he preached about humility and civility, so he practised what he preached, as he graciously allowed one who came into existence just about when he had already begun his ministry to interrogate his work. It communicated volumes!

Devon Dick, who is a significant Jamaican clergyman, over the years has been, as is demonstrated by this collection of sermons, clear in his thinking and committed to the development of the Jamaican voice. Seldom has he been shy to bring his voice to bear on the times within our nation, and he has done so quite avidly through articles and books. This collection of sermons in this volume are insightful and timely, and forms part of this exceptional legacy, adding to the rare yet rich articulation of Jamaican contextual sermons. His courage and tenacity in the pulpit betray him as a truth speaker, and never

AFTERWORD

cause his words to cloud the "Word" in his messages. These sermons are examples of this kind of integrity portrayed by the preacher. They come to life in the hands of the reader as the power of the word, remaining latent until read, gripping the soul, and inspiring transformation. In them, Dick's interpretive skills expertly pivot Christian theology and root it deeply in his understanding of the culture and context of our country, making each sermon poignant and life-changing. Additionally, by his use of the Jamaican New Testament throughout the introduction, Dick demonstrates his appreciation of our culture and expresses a commitment to promulgating and embracing it in the pulpit as well.

The way the work has been sectioned gives credence to the title of this publication, *Preaching in Jamaican Seasons*, and represents important aspects of Revd Dr Dick's preaching ministry:

1. Chapter 1, "Preaching During a Pandemic", aptly opens a magnificent work that reveals the voice of sobriety and grace Revd Dr Dick has been as a pastor and a writer. The unprecedented COVID-19 pandemic has demanded, among many things, a conscious voice of reason and direction, which these sermons provide.
2. The second chapter "Presidential Proclamations" embodies his message to the entire 338 churches of the Jamaica Baptist Union during his two years as its president (2016-2018).
3. Chapter 3, "Special Occasion Sermons", is a demonstration of how Revd Dr Dick freely lends himself to the service of community, and equally brings the truth into those spheres.
4. The fourth chapter, "Home-going Homilies", reveals the friend of the sorrowing and bereaved. In them, he "communes as friend with friend", appreciating life while coming alongside those in pain.
5. The final chapter "Evangelistic Exhortations" closes the work, but is not to be reduced to a "closing statement", for it signals the vast premium Revd Dr Dick has placed on the salvation of human beings.

As I bring my thoughts to a close in this Afterword, may I say a word of challenge to those of us who come to this book as preachers? This work, despite its size, stands tall as a significant challenge for us to be more disciplined in our writing, documenting and publishing of the

Afterword

sermons we preach. It serves as a timeless reminder that our word to the local context quite often can challenge thousands more.

Finally, to the thousands for whom this work will become a source of inspiration and challenge, may you hear in these individual sermons, but also in the work as a whole, the call of God who has been, is and always will be with us.

— Judith Johnson-Grant
Minister of Religion, Jamaica Baptist Union
Health and Faith Researcher, UWI, UTCWI

Bibliography

The Baptist Hymn Book. London: Morris and Gibb Limited, 1962.

Jamaica Baptist Union. *Baptist Preaching in Jamaica: Celebrating Christ for Today (1964-2014).* Kingston: Jamaica Baptist Union, 2015.

Bridgewater, Pamela. "Neutral on Nothing: The Social Activism of the Rev. Dr. B.H. Hester." Fredericksburg: np, 2019.

Brown, Suzanne Francis. *Generational Cycles: A Family of Browns Across a Century of Change,* 2000.

Caribbean Challenge. Kingston: Christian Literature Crusade, January 1988.

Chambers, Donald D. *Transformed by the Deep: Reflections of a Caribbean Priest.* Yellville, Arkansas: Whitehall Publishing, 2017.

Di Jamiekan Nyuu Testament. Kingston: Bible Society of the West Indies, 2012.

Dick, Devon. *Enduring Advocacy for a Better Jamaica: A Collection of Conversations.* Kingston: Arawak publications, 2019.

_____. *Rebellion to Riot: The Jamaican Church in Nation Building.* 2002. Rev. ed. Kingston: Ian Randle Publishers, 2004.

_____. *The Cross and the Machete: Native Baptists of Jamaica: Identity, Ministry and Legacy.* Kingston: Ian Randle Publishers, 2009.

Dumas, Alexandre. *The Three Musketeers.* New York: Sterling Pub., 2007.

Gayle, C.H.L., and W.W. Watty, eds. *The Caribbean Pulpit: An Anthology.* Kingston: np., 1983.

Grasso, Domenico. *Proclaiming God's Message: A Study in the Theology of Preaching.* Notre Dame: University of Notre Dame Press, 1965.

Gregory, Howard K.A. *Journey to the Promised Land: Theological Reflections by Neville W. deSouza on Jamaica's Journey.* Kingston: Ian Randle Publishers, 2019.

BIBLIOGRAPHY

Hastings, S.U. *These Fifty Years*. Aruba: Moravian Church Foundation, 1991.

[The] Jamaica Gazette Supplement, Vol. CXLIII No. 69. April 14, 2020.

Jamaica Observer. "Patients Dying.", August 16, 2019.

King, Martin Luther, Jr. Revd. *Strength to Love*. Boston: Beacon Press, 1963.

Kuck, David W. *Preaching in the Caribbean: Building Up a People for Mission*. Kingston: Faith Works Press, 2007.

Levy, Horace, compiler. *They Cry "Respect"!: Urban Violence and Poverty in Jamaica*. Mona, Jamaica: UWI, 2001.

Locke, John. *Letter Concerning Toleration*. London, 1689.

Osbeck, Kenneth W. *101 Hymn Stories: The Inspiring True Stories Behind 101 Favorite Hymns*. Grand Rapids: Kregel, 1982.

Parker, Joseph. *Prayers and Sermons from the City Pulpit*. 1900 rvsd. ed.; Chattanooga: AMG Publishers, 1996.

Roper, Garnett. *This is the Year of Jubilee*. Kingston: Xpress Litho, 2012.

_____. *Who God Bless No Man Curse: The Blessings of the Blessed Life*. Kingston: Jugaro, 2015.

_____. *Thus Says the Lord. Responding to the Resurgence of Empire: Readings from the Minor Prophets and the Book of Daniel*. Kingston: Jugaro, 2018.

Russell, Horace O. *Five Words of Love*. Kingston: Ebony Christian Books, 1983.

_____. *8 Eight Pathways to Happiness: Living the Be-Attitudes*. Scotts Valley: CreateSpace Independent Publishing Platform, 2011.

_____. *Ten Reasons for Living: Studies in the Lord's Prayer*. Scotts Valley: CreateSpace Independent Publishing Platform, 2011.

Serju, Christopher. "Politicians Perpetuating Slavery – Mitchell." *The Gleaner*, December 6, 2017.

Taylor, Burchell. *The Church Taking Sides: A Contextual Reading of the Letters to the Seven Churches in the Book of Revelation*. Kingston: Bethel Baptist Church, 1995.

Bibliography

———. *The Best of the Attitudes – The Jesus Way: Meditations on the Beatitudes in the Gospel According to Matthew.* Kingston, Caribbean Christian Publications, 2019.

Thame, Camilo, and Maziki Thame. "Porsches, Poverty, Prosperity." *The Gleaner*, Aug. 18, 2019.

Thompson, Robert M, ed. *Mandate for Mission: Do Justice, Love Mercy and Walk Humbly with Your God.* Kingston: Pear Tree Press, 2011.

Tomlin, Carol. *Preach It! Understanding African Caribbean Preaching.* London: SCM, 2018.

Watty, William. *From Shore to Shore: Soundings in Caribbean Theology.* Kingston: n.p. 1981.

www.ingramcontent.com/pod-product-compliance
Lightning Source LLC
Chambersburg PA
CBHW060822190426
43197CB00038B/2184